Courage to Leap & Lead

A Roadmap for Redefining Failure Into Success

CB Bowman-Ottomanelli,
MCEC, BCC, CMC, CVP, CVF

Jones Media Publishing

Courage to Leap & Lead: *A Roadmap for Redefining Failure Into Success*

Written by: CB Bowman-Ottomanelli

Copyright © 2023 by CB Bowman-Ottomanelli, MCEC, BCC, CMC, CVP, CVF

Jones Media Publishing
10645 N. Tatum Blvd. Ste. 200-166
Phoenix, AZ 85028
www.JonesMediaPublishing.com

Printed in the United States of America

ISBN: 978-1-948382-48-9 paperback

Endorsements

"I've worked with many external speakers for large corporate conferences and meetings for many years and highly recommend CB Bowman as an inspirational speaker. She has a fresh and inspiring view of courage and how to implement it into your organization and life. CB is authentic in her mission to help others, both through her speaking engagements and her workshops. She possesses wisdom and grace. Her refreshing approach takes a no blame, no shame approach and uses simple solutions to solve complex problems. CB brings fresh air to the world of speakers; not only is she articulate, she has a great sense of humor that relates to all levels of the organization."

—Dr. Marshall Goldsmith, Thinkers50 Hall of Fame, #1 Leadership Thinker, #1 Exec Coach, #1 NYT Bestselling Author

"CB is relatable, knowledgeable, and inspirational! She conveys powerful insights and establishes a wonderful rapport with any audience. CB's vast reservoir of experience and ability to make relatable connections mark her as a phenomenal speaker and leader! I highly recommend CB Bowman as a keynote speaker who can add substantively to any company's event."

—Brigadier General Dr. Bernard "Bernie" Banks, Principal, Banks Talent Solutions LLC, Associate Dean for Leadership Development and Inclusion, Northwestern University's Kellogg School of Management

"CB is a warm, funny, authentic speaker who creates the space for people to consider topics they might otherwise avoid. Her take on things is refreshing and memorable – she's a gem!"

—Dr. Rita McGrath, Speaker/ Author of "Seeing Around Corners: How to Spot Inflection Points in Business Before They Happen" and "The End of Competitive Advantage: How to Keep Your Strategy Moving as Fast as Your Business"

"CB is a warm, engaging, super smart and sizzling speaker with a depth of knowledge and a great sense of humor. I love sharing the stage with CB. She's a consummate professional, a force of nature and makes everyone around her shine."

—Sally Helgesen, Speaker/ Author "How Women Rise" and "The Female Vision: Women's Real Power at Work"

"It takes a spark to get a fire burning. CB is that spark. She encourages, lights up and warms all those around her. She describes herself as the Courage Consultant and after you have been interviewed by her - like I have - or are fortunate enough to interview her as a subject, as I also have, you will leave with your own courage re-energized. More than a spark, actually, CB radiates like the sun."

—Gina London, CEO and Founder of Language of Leadership and Emmy Award-winning former CNN journalist

"CB instills pure energy, is brave, loyal, and reliable. I am extremely grateful to her for her generous collaboration on our recent AECOP Conference and her inspiring keynote presentation, "The Courage to LEAP first! ...then figure out where you want to land." We wanted to speak about courage in an

especially complex time to make risky decisions and CB brought a motivating, inspiring view and valuable proposals to take action. The conference participants enjoyed her presentation and valued highly positively her contributions. As for me, I feel very fortunate and grateful for having CB in my life."

—Pilar Colilla, Presidenta de AECOP
Asociación de Coaching Ejecutivo y Organizativo

"CB Bowman's gifts as a speaker is a combination of uncanny wisdom, energy, humor, and provocateur. You walk away from her presentations with some fresh perspectives worth contemplating and then putting into practice. And you will remember her infectious good humor."

—Dr. Frank Wagner, Co-Founder of
The Marshall Goldsmith Group

"One of my favorite podcasts out there! There are so many podcasts out there that it is impossible to keep up. But one show that I am always sure never to miss is "CB Bowman Live: Challenges of the C-Suite"! Not only is the show always interesting and educational, but it is also light, fun, and entertaining. CB's mix of wonderful guests, casual and conversational style, and insightful observations make for a winning combination...not only for those in the C-Suite, but for anyone and everyone."

—Dr. Richard E. Boyatzis, Ph.D., author of "Helping People
Change: Coaching with Compassion for Lifelong
Learning and Growth", Case Western Reserve University,
Distinguished University Professor

"If you are looking for a unique and engaging speaker who draws on extensive experience and insight in a way that is both practical and encouraging, then CB Bowman is for you.

She helps others tackle difficult topics in a warm and open way that cultivates aha moments and fosters constructive action. What I think of as 'everyday courage' requires the courage to say yes and also the courage to say no – and CB helps people appropriately implement both."

—Dr. Sim Sitkin Duke University Michael W. Krzyzewski University Professor Michael W. Krzyzewski University Professor, Director, Behavioral Science and Policy Center, Social Science Research Institute Social Science Research Institute, Faculty Director, Fuqua/ Coach K Center on Leadership and Ethics Faculty Director

"Unapologetically powerful! I love CB's unabashedly passionate, probing and provocative interview style. Of all the many podcasts and media I've worked with, CB gets to the heart of important issues in the C-Suite and of our world today."

—Amii Barnard-Bahn, JD, CEO, Author of "Promotability Index®"

"CB Bowman is genuine, inspiring and relatable, qualities you most want to have in a keynote speaker. Her insight, caring and passion come through loudly in her talks and leave people wanting more."

—Howard Prager, President Advance Learning Group; Author Make Someone's Day: Becoming a Memorable Leader in Work and Life

"I had the opportunity to meet CB while I was part of the organizing team of the 10th AECOP International Executive Coaching Congress. CB shared in the Congress a really inspiring keynote presentation on Courage and Fear Management. I was

fascinated by her generosity and integrity in the relationship with her, being able to generate immense trust with her humility and enthusiasm. CB has a great capacity for empathic listening and is able to transform what is difficult into apparently simple and logical ideas. She is an excellent communicator, who generated empowering and positive energy in the attendees, so they were aware of the power in all of us we have to improve in our business and in our lives. It has been wonderful to meet her and to be inspired by her humanity, professionalism, and passion for people."

—Noelia Bermúdez Mayora,
Internacional de personas Coaching Ejecutivo
(International Executive Coach)

CB is an inspirational speaker and thought leader. It was wonderful to have CB as part of our Global Equality in Leadership Summit last month. I highly recommend CB's work."

—Simon Haigh, CEO The Growth Strategist -
MBA, BA (Hons) LawEO

CB always sees beyond the surface and towards the future. If you are looking for a speaker who can help you scale up and step up in order to identify income streams, look no further. CB is the one."

—Dr. Ana Melikian, Host of the "Mindset Zone"
Podcast, Keynote Speaker "The Happiness Fallacy"

"Thank you so much for speaking today! You inspire me and I know you have inspired our audience as well! You are magnifique!"

—Caroline Boyce, THE CFO Leadership Council,
North Andover, MA, Diversity, Equity and
Inclusion Director and National Membership Manager

As an expert in leadership, I can tell you that Bowman's book is an outstanding resource to anyone seeking to improve their skills and outlook both on work and on life!"

Gregg Ward MCEC, BCC Founder/ Executive Director
The Center for Respectful Leadership
Author of the Award-Winning,
Bestselling Business Fable The Respectful Leader

"Among the many qualities that I can use to describe CB, as a speaker and as a consultant are "Life Learner" and "Intuitive Creator". In every single conversation, I walk away with deep insights and a thirst for more time with her. Her depth of wisdom and her sheer desire to know more is what sets her apart from the many Executive Gurus in her field. She never enters a conversation ill-prepared, and she never leaves one making you feel as though you were the only one that learned. She is generous beyond reason with her time and knowledge. And, she never fails to spark one's excitement to move toward desired goals with a full heart and a clear mind."

—Dr. Mirella De Civita, MCEC,
President of Papillon MDC Inc. |
Founder of Grand Heron International Inc.

"Courage is a powerful thing and so is this podcast! Having the honor of being in conversation with CB Bowman, was a highlight of my 2022. CB is a master at the art of conversation, and goes deep with each guest on how to lead with courage. If you want an insight on how we can flex the courage muscle and become better leaders, CB will show you how."

—*Tricia Brouk CEO The Big Talk*

**CB Bowman-Ottomanelli, MCEC, BCC, CMC, MBA;
Courage Implementation Coach**
CEO Courage Consulting
CEO Association of Corporate Executive Coaches

Dedication

**Dedicated to all who told me
"No" or "You Can't."**

Acknowledgements

Ann Daw:
Who said how can I help?

Anthony J Ottomanelli:
Who said I love you!

Barbara Singer:
Who motivated me to stay focused!

Brandon Lloyd:
Who said you need to write a book!

Dr. Brian Schwartz:
Who said to me the naysayers are not worth a warm bowl of spit.

Doreen Stephens:
Who said I'm proud of you!

Dr. Frank Wagner, Sally Helgesen and Cynthia Burnham:
Who introduced me to game changers.

Howard Morgan:
Who encouraged me to go for the gold.

Dr. Marshall Goldsmith:
Who said what do you want to be known for?

Miriam Clark, JD:
Who said we've got this.

Pilar Colilla Rubio:
Who said you are the most courageous person I know.

Thank you all for being part of my journey.

Foreword

A Guru Speaks:
Dr. Marshall Goldsmith

In this book, CB Bowman tackles the elephant in the room. In the midst of five current pandemics – COVID-19, economics, mental health, environment, and social justice – there is a need for courage to be displayed by everyone more than ever before. But few of us know how to recognize and implement courage in an organizational environment, or how to use it to fulfill our lives.

Bowman, the CEO and founder of the Association of Corporate Executive Coaches, is a master level corporate executive coach and consultant. A brilliant and engaging keynote speaker on this topic, she has been helping leaders and teams recover from dysfunctional work environments that paralyze them in making decisions for fear of failure. She explains saving courage through anecdotes and practical tools, including her seven-step roadmap, fishbone charts, SWOT analysis, and more. This book illustrates how we can have the courage to create successful solutions and avoid causing shame, embarrassment, a loss of self-worth, and a loss of pride. Most importantly, this is a guide to building a legacy of success inside and outside of the workplace.

Bowman provides a roadmap that allows us to implement courage on both micro and macro levels. Not only does she break down the difference between the two types of courage, she also helps the reader understand how to redefine failure and, ultimately, how to use lessons learned from failure to generate future success.

She proposes that failure is synonymous with a university education for success. We must take failure and dissect it so that the outcomes become part of the framework to lead us to success for the next go-around. Bowman helps us to see that courage is not the elephant in the room, but rather we need to see it in terms of micro-steps to applaud ourselves each day. Microcourage© is not the person who is running into a burning building to save a child or jumping into a swimming pool to save a dog when they can't swim. Those are acts of Macrocourage©. Instead, she presents the idea of applauding and rewarding ourselves for our daily acts of Microcourage©, such as supporting one's convictions, asking for a raise, launching a new product, or supporting social justice in or outside of the office. It could even be getting up in the morning and going to work to face a hostile environment. These are examples of acts of courage that fuel our progress forward over time and create larger change for our lives.

Bowman's stories about her life challenges and rewards will invigorate and inspire you toward a path of discovery. They will also enable you to recognize and respect the courage that you have in yourself and help you to be aware and appreciate the courage displayed by others. Knowing that courage is rarely spoken of in this way, Bowman provides a seven-step roadmap to help each of us discover the courage within, helping us to utilize it for the greater good. We no longer have to sit on the sidelines and say, 'I wish I had the courage.'

Dr. Marshall Goldsmith
Thinkers50 #1 Executive Coach
New York Times Bestselling Author of *The Earned Life*,
Triggers, and *What Got You Here Won't Get You There*

Table of Contents

Introduction

A mid several pandemics (economic, environmental, mental health, social justice, and COVID-19) and uncertainty about the future, leaders must take extra measures to instill confidence in their employees. However, a significant danger exists when a company's culture stimulates the lack of confidence to make courageous decisions. Courageous leadership requires a mindset shift from the top to the bottom of an organization. This book provides a roadmap for individuals and organizations to transform themselves by implementing a courageous mindset and enabling everyone to adapt quickly in an ever-changing environment.

"Fear is looking into your mind and seeing nothing. Courage is looking at your mind and seeing too much."
—CB Bowman-Ottomanelli

This book takes you on a path to discovery. By giving examples of my life as a black woman who experienced Malcolm X, Martin Luther King Jr., Stokely Carmichael, Angela Davis, and many more, and by sharing my experiences in turning failures into victories, it is my gift to you to have the Courage to Leap & Lead; to leap from the fires of life into the success you richly deserve in all parts of your life, be it personal or business.

The deeply personal and business stories I share with you are samples of Microcourage© which, together supported my leap into success as a business person and they supported my leap into success in the personal aspects of my life.

An essential aspect in the book *Courage to Leap & Lead: A Roadmap for Redefining Failure Into Success* introduces the term Microcourage©.

> *"Great things are done by a series of small things brought together."*
>
> **—Vincent Van Gogh**

Microcourage© asks you to accept a new constrict regarding the interpretation of failure. Failure becomes *the academic pathway to success* when viewed and analyzed through the lens of Microcourage©. Through this lens, you will be able to identify and celebrate lessons learned in failure to resurrect the situation, like the phoenix rising from the ashes. **Micro**courage© asks you to respect and celebrate small acts of courage, the cumulation of which equals **Macro**courage©.

Courage to Leap & Lead: A Roadmap for Redefining Failure Into Success, is designed to help you develop the skills and mindset that set courageous leaders apart.

This book introduces you to key concepts, including the seven steps of **implementing** courageous leadership, influence and engagement styles, and tools for leading change. You'll also learn about the behaviors related to courage in the workplace.

For the first time, a roadmap has been designed, which gives you a system for using simple solutions to solve complex problems, which is the secret sauce for turning failure into success. ***This book takes you on a path to discovery.***

SECTION 1

~

In the Beginning

*"You gain strength, courage and confidence
by every experience in which you really stop
to look fear in the face. You are able to say to yourself,
'I have lived through this horror. I can take the next
thing that comes along.' You must do the thing
you think you cannot do."*

**— Eleanor Roosevelt, *You Learn
by Living: Eleven Keys for
a More Fulfilling Life***

Dyslexia the Stimuli Behind My Courage

I believe that I was forced to be courageous as a Dyslexic. Courage is often associated with facing and overcoming complex challenges, and individuals with dyslexia embody this trait in many ways. Dyslexia is a neurodevelopmental disorder that affects reading and writing skills and other cognitive functions such as memory, processing speed, and spatial awareness. Yet, despite the many challenges that dyslexic individuals face in their academic and personal lives, they often demonstrate remarkable courage and resilience in the face of adversity. We will explore the links between courage and dyslexia and how dyslexic individuals can use their strengths to overcome challenges and achieve success.

One of the main ways dyslexic individuals demonstrate courage is by facing their learning difficulties head-on. Dyslexia can be frustrating and discouraging, as it can affect a person's ability to read and write, which are fundamental skills required in many aspects of life. These individuals often demonstrate remarkable perseverance and determination in their efforts. They may seek out specialized tutoring or educational programs, invest extra time and effort into their studies, or develop coping strategies that help them navigate the challenges of their condition. Facing one's limitations and working to overcome them can be daunting. However, dyslexic individuals often rise to the challenge and demonstrate a level of determination and tenacity that is truly inspiring.

Another way in which dyslexic individuals demonstrate courage is by challenging the stigma and misconceptions that surround this neurodevelopmental. Unfortunately, there is still a great deal of misunderstanding and ignorance surrounding dyslexia, and many people continue to view it as a sign of intellectual inferiority or laziness. However, dyslexic individuals are often quick to challenge these misconceptions and advocate for greater understanding and support. They may share their stories and experiences, educate others about the condition, and work to break down barriers and promote inclusivity. This response takes great courage, as it can be challenging to speak out against ignorance and prejudice, especially when it affects one's sense of self-worth and identity.

In addition to these external displays of courage, challenging individuals demonstrate great inner strength and resilience. Dyslexia can be challenging, affecting many aspects of one's life, including self-esteem, social relationships, and career prospects. These individuals often develop strong self-awareness and self-acceptance, allowing them to thrive despite challenges. They may learn to appreciate their unique strengths and abilities, create a sense of humor and resilience in the face of setbacks, and find ways to leverage their Condition as a source of creativity and innovation.

Finally, it is essential to note that dyslexic individuals often demonstrate great courage in their willingness to seek out and accept help from others. Dyslexia can be a complex and multifaceted condition, often requiring a multidisciplinary approach to treatment and support. Dyslexic individuals with Affected individuals may work with tutors, therapists, educators, or other professionals to develop their skills and strategies to succeed. They may also seek peer support groups, online communities, or other networks offering guidance, encouragement, and understanding. This requires humility and vulnerability, as it can be difficult to admit one's limitations and rely on others for support.

The difficulty with defining courage is the same as when the medical profession is trying to define Dyslexia; courage means different things to different people; it takes on many forms depending on several factors, such as values, beliefs, experience, and emotions. We must acknowledge the difference between a person who needs the courage to deal with drugs or alcohol versus a person coping with Dyslexia (see chapter: "What Happens When You Cannot Pass the Entrance Exam?") or the courage needed from a person dealing with an unsuccessful product launch.One type of courage is not greater than the other; it is just different, and different behaviors may be required.

"Courage is in the eye of the beholder."

—CB Bowman

The numerous description discrepancies for the word courage can be compared to definitions for the word Dyslexia. For those with Dyslexia, the "Dyslexia" is a brain-based learning disability that affects a person's reading ability, writing ability, and in some cases, ability to speak.

However, for those with Dyslexia, the disability affects a wide range of people and produces different symptoms with varying degrees of severity, making consistent diagnoses difficult.

The Diagnostic and Statistical Manual of Mental Disorders (DSM), first published in 1952, is the handbook used by healthcare professionals in the United States and much of the world as the authoritative guide in diagnosing mental disorders. In this classic guide, Dyslexia was not recognized until the fourth version, released in 1994. However, researchers have studied learning difficulties and people with Dyslexia since the 17th century.

On balance, the term dyslexia now appears well-established if not permanently embedded in professional and public vocabularies. However, precision in its definition(s) remains elusive; Dyslexia is the object of progressive and accelerating research. Therefore, the new knowledge is expected to illuminate the variables encompassed by the concept. Definitional refinement and modification will be forthcoming. At play in all of this will be sociocultural factors.

Dyslexia is, at one level, but a word. As a word, the question becomes what meanings will be ascribed to it. New knowledge about Dyslexia, including shifting attitudes, assure that new ascriptions will be forthcoming. Nevertheless, its future definitions are, in some measure, problematic (Tønnessen, 1997). For researchers, the term is likely to function as a general umbrella concept under which more differentiating and rigorously formulated constructs are absorbed. At the same time, there will likely be some who will take positions at variance with any emerging research consensus. This construct will ensure the continuation, at some level, of the controversy that has marked the term's history (Hanford, 2018).

The definition of courage appears to suffer the same "malady." *Courage as a behavior becomes what meanings are ascribed to it.* There is general agreement that courage involves making a decision despite concern or fear of retribution. However, in most cases, the word "courage" has been aggrandized so that it appears unattainable to most. In this book, we will focus on courage that – *for most* – is more obtainable.

In this book, the concept of **Microcourage**© is presented. It is defined as small acts of courage that can be applied in the workplace and life that lead to a goal. Importantly, steps are presented to you the reader to support you to implement Microcourage© as a process that leads to success. For some, Microcourage© might be getting out of bed in the morning and going to work. You may wonder how that is courageous. Well, consider a person diagnosed with secondary-progressive Multiple Sclerosis (MS) performing that same act of getting out of bed in the morning. **Does that change your view of the term courage when used here?**

Consider Michael J. Fox continuing to advocate for those with Parkinson's disease while he is progressively worsening himself with this malady. Alternatively, consider people faced with racism, hostility, or bullying in their work environment going to work every day. Then there is courage at work, which can be seen when speaking up to no longer be treated without respect for their contributions.

Many have tried to define courage throughout the years. Merriam-Webster defines the meaning of courage as the "mental or moral strength to venture, persevere, and withstand danger, fear, or difficulty." Dictionary.com defines it as "the quality of mind or spirit that enables a person to face difficulty, danger, pain, without fear; bravery." Furthermore, the Cambridge English Dictionary states that courage is "the ability to control fear and to be willing to deal with something dangerous, difficult, or unpleasant."

In the *Psychology of Courage: Modern Research on Ancient Virtue*, published in 2002, courage is broken down into areas of philosophy, social sciences, literature, and lexicons.

Courage Defined by Philosophers Over the Years

Courage is a "disposition to confront fear
(rather than being fearless)" and... It is essential
to advancing the agent's good and the common good
of human communities."

—Per Roald Bauhn,
Swedish philosopher

"Courage is the ability to confront, master, and
overcome fear, which assumes that they either exist
or might reasonably exist and the risk that
we incur must be in proportion to the end we seek."

—André Comte-Sponville, French philosopher

"Courage is the capacity to risk harm or danger to oneself."

—Alasdair MacIntyre, Scottish-American philosopher

Courage Defined by Social Scientists Over the Years

According to Stephen Jay Gould, "moral courage" is the intersection of principles, danger, and endurance. "Moral courage is a commitment to moral principles, awareness of the danger involved in supporting those principles, and a willing endurance of that danger."

Courage defines by Psychologist Over the Years

The Psychology of Courage: Modern Research on an Ancient Virtue cites that a courageous act in an organization includes five essential properties:

1. Member has free choice to act
2. Member experience is a significant risk
3. Member assesses the risk as reasonable
4. Members contemplate an act
5. Member proceeds despite fear with mindful action

Uncertainty and fear have bubbled to the surface due to five pandemics colliding. The result is that our system thinking for solving fear has gone askew and has wreaked havoc on our courage. Through the use of Microcourage© system thinking, we can abort what is stopping us from reaching our goals.

In most cases, courage is defined concerning massive fear and large-scale danger, making it seem unattainable by the masses. So let us revisit the meaning of courage to make it more inclusive.

Courage in the Workplace

Courage is a quality we can all show in the workplace, one of the top qualities of a great leader. It gives one the strength to develop their potential and step up when needed. A person might not know what they are stepping into until they take action, but a courageous leader says, "I am going for it," anyhow. Courage involves taking risks and facing difficult situations and people fearlessly. In addition, courage is being true to one's values, regardless of what others think or say.

Asking for a promotion or raise, standing up for your values, introducing a new product or service, and confronting an issue head-on are all workplace courage. The courage needed to have one's own opinion and speak up with respect and conviction is enormous; all of these examples are actions of **Micro**courage©, as we are not talking **Macro**courage© such as whistleblowing or risking your life to save someone or something. Courage resides in the ability to "*be fierce and fearless, to be more, to step out, stand tall to know that you are invincible,*" stand up for what you believe in and speak loudly enough for others to hear– even when the opinions are unpopular or may cause confrontation.

On a grander scale in the workplace, courage combines company culture, leadership and values, and personal mindset. It does not happen by accident. "*Courage is the foundational skill for managing change in today's business environment.*"

"It is not the size of the dog in the fight, but the size of the fight in the dog that matters."

—Mark Twain

Courageousness can be seen in creating a plan and a strategy and achieving a goal. Taking a leap of faith can be frightening, but it does not mean you have to go it alone or blindly without a plan, strategy, or set goals.

Levels of Courage in the Workplace

The levels of courage in the workplace include the courage to grow, learn and change, the courage to confront those who threaten your integrity and self-esteem, the courage to question authority, the courage to take risks, the courage to be yourself, and lastly, the courage to leap.

Levels of courage include bravery, fearlessness, and boldness. In the workplace, we all encounter situations that require us to be courageous, some as simple as asking for a raise and others as difficult as terminating an employee, whistleblowing, or leaving a position. Being brave entails doing what is right, even difficult or frightening. Fearlessness means not feeling afraid in a specific situation. Finally, boldness denotes being confident enough to express oneself through speech and actions regardless of the potential outcome, no matter how difficult. *"It is important to understand that courage is the ability to face a fear as defined by you."*

The courage to leap and lead is rooted in personal integrity, creativity, and relentless communication. In today's world, we are constantly faced with situations where the action is needed, and hesitation can be crippling. Examples can be seen in the pandemic we currently face. For example, with Covid, should we get vaccinated or risk the exposure and spreading of the disease, or do we risk having a physical reaction to the drug? With social justice, do we speak up in favor of acts of social justice in the workplace and risk being shunned, or do we repent in silence? With the environment, how do we support methods to prevent further climate change and not appear to be obsessive? For economics, what is our part in the economic crisis, and what part do we play in an economic collapse? How and when do we step in to support those struggling with mental health?

Research About Courage in the Workplace

The latest research shows that leaders who display courage, regardless of whether their actions are met with success or failure, are more likely to inspire and motivate others. Courage is what makes a true leader. The power is in learning to harness the courage you need to grow and lead in today's rapidly changing workplace. This critical leadership quality trickles down and inspires others to take action and make change happen. Surprisingly these leaders are not afraid to show vulnerability or share their flaws with others. Instead, they take risks, push the limits, and dive into new experiences – often without knowing what will happen next.

Research on courage in the workplace reveals that people experience fear, but fear is only a barrier when they allow it to stop them from taking action. In the coming chapters, you will find tools to help you mitigate fear and live a more creative, productive, and courageous life.

The workplace is changing. Embracing change requires agility and risk-taking, but failure can be costly when you do not make the right decision. In Rita McGrath's book *Seeing Around Corners How to Spot Inflection Points in Business Before They Happen*, she helps readers understand how and where to look for opportunities for long-term success by being aware of times of significant change. Using this wisdom from observation, history, and research allows individuals and organizations to be in the crosshairs of potential success. However, It takes extraordinary Microcourage© to be aware, research, and use history to be bold and fearless to produce change.

Ten Specific Ways to Become a More Courageous Leader

Organizations must have courageous leaders, regardless of size or industry. The behavior generally includes making tough decisions, taking calculated risks, and standing up for what is right, even in the face of opposition. Courageous leaders inspire their team members, earn their trust, and build a culture of excellence that drives success.

1. **Embrace vulnerability:** Courageous leaders understand that vulnerability is not a weakness but a strength. They are willing to admit their mistakes, share their fears, and ask for help when needed. By embracing vulnerability, you show your team members that being imperfect is okay and that everyone has room to grow and learn.

2. **Communicate with transparency:** Leaders who are transparent in their communication earn the trust of their team members. Be honest about your vision, goals, and challenges. Share your progress and setbacks, and involve your team members in decision-making. When you communicate transparently, your team members feel valued, respected, and engaged.

3. **Take calculated risks:** Courageous leaders understand that taking risks is crucial to innovation and growth. However, they do not take reckless risks that could jeopardize the organization's stability. Instead, they take calculated risks aligned with the organization's values, goals, and resources. Taking calculated risks demonstrates your willingness to explore new opportunities and push boundaries.

4. **Stand up for what is right:** Courageous leaders have a solid moral compass and are not afraid to stand up

for what is right, even when it is unpopular or risky. As a result, they create a culture of integrity, respect, and accountability and hold themselves and others accountable for their actions. By standing up for what is right, you inspire your team members to do the same and build a culture of trust and excellence.

5. **Embrace diversity and inclusion:** Courageous leaders understand the value of diversity and inclusion and actively promote them in their organizations. They create a safe and inclusive environment where everyone feels valued, respected, and heard. By embracing diversity and inclusion, you foster innovation, creativity, and empathy and build a stronger and more resilient team.

6. **Foster a growth versus a punitive mindset:** Courageous leaders believe that everyone has the potential to grow and learn, and they foster a growth mindset in their organizations. They encourage their team members to embrace challenges, learn from their mistakes, and continuously improve their skills and knowledge. By fostering a growth mindset, you create a continuous learning and improvement culture that drives innovation and growth.

7. **Lead by example:** Courageous leaders lead by example and set the tone for their organizations. They embody the values and behaviors they expect from their team members and hold themselves to the same high standards. By leading by example, you inspire your team members to follow your lead and build a culture of excellence.

8. **Foster open communication:** Courageous leaders foster open communication in their organizations and encourage their team members to speak up and share their ideas, concerns, and feedback. As a result, they

create a safe and supportive environment where everyone feels comfortable expressing themselves. By fostering open communication, you promote collaboration,
creativity, and engagement and build a more connected
and productive team.

9. **Take care of yourself:** Courageous leaders understand
the importance of self-care and prioritize their health and
well-being. As a result, they manage their stress, prioritize their time, and maintain a healthy work-life balance.
By caring for yourself, you model healthy behavior for
your team members and create a culture that values well-
being and balance.

10. **Seek feedback and support:** Courageous leaders seek
feedback and support from their team members, peers,
and mentors. They are open to constructive criticism and
use it to improve their leadership.

Courage as the Missing Link for Increasing Capacity in Organizations

Courage is not just crucial for leaders; it is also a critical factor
for increasing capacity in organizations. Empowering employees
to take risks and pursue new ideas can lead to innovation,
resilience, and improved communication.

Innovation is one of the primary drivers of organizational success.
However, innovation requires a culture of psychological safety.
Employees must feel they can take risks and share their ideas without
fear of retribution or ridicule. When employees feel safe to take risks,
it can lead to breakthroughs and increased capacity. Nevertheless,
creating a psychological safety culture requires courageous leaders
willing to take risks and encourage their teams to do the same.

The leaders who promote innovation in their organizations
also inspire their teams to think outside the box. They encourage

their employees to question the status quo and pursue new ideas. Employees feeling empowered to take risks can lead to a more engaged workforce invested in the organization's success. Innovation also helps organizations stay ahead of the competition by finding new and better ways to serve their customers.

In addition to promoting innovation, courage also helps organizations build resilience. Resilience is the ability to adapt to change and recover from adversity. When organizations are resilient, they can better weather challenges and become more assertive on the other side. However, resilience requires the courage to face difficult situations and the determination to persevere.

Leaders who model resilience can inspire their teams to do the same. When employees see their leaders persevering in the face of adversity, it can motivate them to do the same. Resilience also helps organizations avoid being blindsided by unexpected challenges. By preparing for potential challenges and developing contingency plans, organizations can be better equipped to handle whatever comes their way.

Effective communication is another critical factor for organizational success. However, communication breakdowns can lead to misunderstandings and missed opportunities. Courageous leaders who are willing to speak up and address issues can help prevent these breakdowns from occurring. By promoting open and honest communication, leaders can help their teams work more effectively and avoid costly mistakes.

Those leaders who prioritize effective communication also create a culture of accountability. When employees feel responsible for their actions and are willing to speak up when they see something that needs to be addressed, it can help prevent minor issues from becoming more significant problems. This kind of communication also helps build trust among team members, which can lead to a more cohesive and effective workforce.

Finally, courage can help organizations create a sense of purpose and mission. When those at the top of the organization and departments are willing to take risks and pursue bold goals, it can inspire their teams to do the same. Organizations can harness the power of their collective energy and talent to achieve great things by creating a shared sense of purpose and mission. This focus can increase capacity and a sense of pride and satisfaction among employees, increasing their motivation and commitment to the organization.

In conclusion, courage is the missing link for increasing capacity in organizations. By fostering innovation, promoting resilience, improving communication, and creating a sense of purpose and mission, courageous leaders can inspire their teams to achieve great things. However, courage must be balanced with other critical factors and developed over time. Organizations that value courage and create a culture of innovation and risk-taking are likelier to thrive in today's fast-paced and ever-changing business landscape. With courage as the foundation, organizations can achieve their full potential and create a culture of excellence that inspires employees and customers.

The Relationship Between Courage and Workplace Stress or Anxiety

The lack of courage in the workplace can significantly impact employees' stress and anxiety levels. In today's fast-paced business environment, where employees are often expected to meet tight deadlines, complete multiple tasks, and navigate complex relationships with colleagues, courage has never been more critical. However, despite its importance, many employees struggle to exhibit courage in the workplace, which can severely affect their well-being.

Stress is a natural response to challenging situations; the workplace is no exception. When employees face a difficult task or situation, stress can help them rise to the challenge and perform at their best. However, when stress becomes chronic, it can have serious adverse effects on mental and physical health.

- One of the main reasons why stress levels in the workplace are so high is the lack of courage among employees. Many people are afraid to speak up, ask for help, or stand up for their beliefs, leading to frustration, inadequacy, and hopelessness.

- Two of the most common workplace stress causes are fear of failure and termination. Many employees fear taking risks, making decisions, or putting themselves out there because they fear what might happen if they fail. This fear can be paralyzing, preventing employees from stepping outside their comfort zones and taking on new challenges. When employees are too afraid to take risks, they are more likely to stay stuck in the same rut, repeating the same tasks and routines daily. This lack of variety and excitement can lead to boredom, burnout, and stress.

Another factor that contributes to workplace stress is the fear of conflict. Many employees fear speaking their minds or expressing their opinions because they fear how others react. This fear of conflict can prevent employees from expressing their ideas, asking for help, or advocating for themselves. When employees are afraid to speak up, they are more likely to keep their thoughts and feelings to themselves, leading to isolation, frustration, and anger. This fear can also lead to a breakdown in communication, which can exacerbate existing conflicts and create new ones. Sadly, it can most definitely affect the employee's health.

In addition to stress, the lack of courage in the workplace can also lead to anxiety. Anxiety is a feeling of unease, such as worry or fear, that can be mild or severe. When employees face difficult situations in the workplace, they may experience anxiety as they try to navigate these challenges. For example, they may fear making mistakes, losing their job, or failing to meet expectations. These feelings of anxiety can be overwhelming, preventing employees from performing at their best.

The impact of anxiety on the workplace, is significant. When employees experience high anxiety levels they are more likely to take sick days, be less productive, and make mistakes. This situation can lead to lower morale, decreased job satisfaction, and a negative impact on the overall culture of the workplace. In addition, anxiety can have long-term effects on an employee's health and well-being, including depression, sleep disturbances, physical health problems, and substance abuse.

Employees need to develop the courage to face difficult situations in the workplace. This courage can help reduce stress and anxiety, increase job satisfaction, and improve mental and physical health. One of the best ways to develop courage is to identify and overcome fears. This realization step may involve taking small risks, practicing assertiveness, and seeking support from others.

In addition to working on personal growth, employers can also play a role in reducing stress and anxiety in the workplace. Reducing stress and anxiety can involve creating a supportive work environment and promoting open communication.

Ten Specific Ways to Identify an Unhealthy Lack of Courage in the Workplace

There is a fine line between a healthy lack of courage and an unhealthy one. When employees lack the courage to the point of being unhealthy, it can have a negative impact on their performance, as well as the performance of the organization as a whole.

Here are ten specific ways to identify an unhealthy lack of courage in the workplace:

1. **Fear of speaking up:** When employees are afraid to speak up and express their opinions, it can indicate an unhealthy lack of courage. This concern over speaking up can lead to missed collaboration, innovation, and problem-solving opportunities.

2. **Lack of initiative:** Employees who lack the courage to take the initiative and solve problems can be a significant issue in the workplace. This can lead to a need for more progress and growth in the organization.

3. **Inability to take risks:** In the current business environment, taking risks is necessary for growth and innovation. However, employees afraid to take risks can hinder progress and stifle creativity.

4. **Avoiding conflict:** Conflict avoidance can indicate an unhealthy lack of courage. Employees who are afraid to address issues and disputes can lead to resentment, mistrust, and a lack of productivity.

5. **Resistance to change:** Resistance is often a sign of an unhealthy lack of courage. Employees afraid of change can resist new ideas, processes, and technologies, leading to a lack of growth and innovation.

6. **Inability to make decisions:** When employees lack the courage to make decisions, it can lead to delays and missed opportunities, resulting in a lack of progress and growth for the organization.

7. **Lack of accountability:** Employees who are afraid to take responsibility for their actions and decisions can be

a significant issue in the workplace. This fear can lead to a lack of trust and accountability within the organization.

8. **Inability to learn from mistakes:** Employees who are afraid to make mistakes and learn from them can be a significant issue in the workplace. This inability can lead to missed opportunities for growth and development.

9. **Lack of confidence:** When employees lack the confidence to take on new challenges and responsibilities, it can indicate an unhealthy lack of courage. This lack of confidence can lead to missed personal and professional growth opportunities.

10. **Lack of empathy:** Courage requires empathizing with others and understanding their perspectives. Employees who lack empathy can be more focused on their own needs and desires than the needs of others. In addition, the lack of empathy can lead to a lack of collaboration and teamwork in the workplace.

Identifying an unhealthy lack of courage in the workplace requires managers to be attentive to the behaviors and attitudes of their employees. When employees lack the courage to speak up, take risks, and make difficult decisions, it can have a negative impact on their performance, as well as the performance of the organization as a whole. Managers can create a more productive and innovative workplace by addressing these issues and encouraging employees to be more courageous. However, it is essential to recognize that some employees may need additional support and training to overcome their fears and develop the courage required to succeed.

Ten Specific Ways to Become a More Courageous Person at Work

Being courageous in the workplace can be difficult, especially when you're used to following the pack. However, being courageous can help you stand out from the crowd, gain respect from your colleagues, and achieve greater success.

Here are ten specific ways to become a more courageous person at work and stop following the pack:

1. **Speak up in meetings:** Be bold and express your opinion, even if it's different from everyone else's. Your unique perspective might be needed to solve a <u>problem or make a breakthrough.</u>

2. **Take on challenging projects:** Only sometimes go for the easy option, or stick to what you know. Take on challenging tasks that push you out of your comfort zone and help you grow.

3. **Be willing to fail:** Failure is part of the learning process; it takes courage to try something new and risk not succeeding. Embrace failure as a learning opportunity and use it to propel you forward.

4. **Stand up for what you believe in:** If you feel strongly about something, don't be afraid to stand up for it. Whether it's a workplace policy or a decision being made by your team, speak up and make your voice heard.

5. **Take calculated risks:** Don't be reckless, but don't be afraid to take calculated risks. If you have an idea that you believe in, take the time to do your research and make a plan before presenting it to your team.

6. **Be proactive:** Don't wait for opportunities; create them yourself. Be proactive in seeking out new challenges and taking on more responsibility.

7. **Learn to say no:** Don't be a pushover. If something doesn't align with your values or you feel uncomfortable with a request, learn to say no. It can be challenging, but it's essential to setting boundaries and standing up for yourself.

8. **Be authentic:** Don't try to be someone you're not. Be true to yourself and your values, and don't compromise them to fit in or please others.

9. **Take ownership of your mistakes:** When you make a mistake, take ownership of it and learn from it. Don't try to shift the blame onto others or make excuses. It takes courage but shows integrity and accountability.

10. **Be a leader, not a follower:** Sometimes, go along with the crowd. Be a leader and set an example for others to follow. Stand up for what you believe in, even if it's not the popular opinion.

Becoming a more courageous person at work requires a willingness to step outside your comfort zone and take risks. It involves speaking up, taking ownership of your mistakes, and being true to yourself and your values. By following the aforementioned ten specific ways to become more courageous, you can **stop following the pack and achieve tremendous success.**

Why Me?

"I never lose. I either win or learn."

—Nelson Mandela

"I am not courageous!" I'd say whenever someone told me, I had courage. I was in denial partially because I never entirely understood what it meant to *have* courage. Although it was something other people had, it looked more like the 9/11 first responders. To top it off, I had the classic case of imposter syndrome — a collection of feelings of inadequacy that persist despite evident success. "Imposters" suffer from chronic self-doubt and intellectual fraudulence that override feelings of success or external proof of competence. And the final reason was that I am a black woman who was focused on survival in a white world, doing what I needed to survive, and I was not focused on being courageous, especially in the way we traditionally defined courage.

So, how and when did my thinking change?

On November 19, 2021, I received an email from my dear friend Pilar Colilla, the president of AECOP España (Asociación Española de Coaching Ejecutivo y Organizativo), asking me if I would be the keynote speaker for her 2021 AECOP International Congress of Executive Coaching Conference. Pilar is a member of my association—the Association of Corporate Executive Coaches (ACEC); consequently, I immediately agreed without asking for details.

During our first meeting to discuss the conference, I asked Pilar if she'd like me to discuss being an executive coach, given that was our shared field of interest. I was surprised when she said "no." Being a black woman, and not long after the killing of George Flloyd, I asked her next if she would like me to speak about DEI. However, she again said no! I was now perplexed. I then said what would you like for me to talk about? Her response was "courage." I was shocked. *"But I don't know anything about courage!" I said. That's when Pilar said, "CB you are the most courageous person I know."* My first thought was, how do I get out of doing this speech? But I was stuck; I had already agreed to speak. I had to come up with something! Magically, when I sat down to write my speech, my fingers took over the keyboard as I thought about my life; the words came along with the realization that I had been courageous all my life. I realized that for so many years, people were correct in telling me I was courageous. Imagine that!

I started thinking about significant events in my life where others thought, "wow, she is either nuts or courageous!" Then, I realized that over the years, I had developed a mental roadmap to help me be courageous, and I had used this roadmap in business and my personal life to propel my success.

I always thought I leaped first and then figured out where I would land. It had become my motto. To the outsider, this is true, but the reality was that I had mastered this seven-step roadmap so that it had become automatic in my head and that while it appeared that I was using my motto, I was using the Microcourage© roadmap.

The Seven Steps of Microcourage©

1. EXERT: Step out of the quagmire.
2. EXPLORE: Courage to examine any external blocks getting in your way.

3. EXAMINE: Courage to inspect and identify internal road-blocks and triggers.

4. EXPRESS: Courage to speak out.

5. ENGAGE: Courage to accept help, to listen, and to acknowledge the support you receive.

6. EXECUTE: Courage to be wrong, courage to be right.

7. RESURGE: Courage to stand up, stand alone, and try again.

As we move forward in this book, I will take you through each of the seven steps with stories that are inspirational, funny, sad, or may appear to be crazy. Your homework is to use each stage and the tools I'll provide for business or in your life and **notate what you have learned.**

Microcourage©

"Microcourage© is the mindset to make a decision to 'act' or not to 'act' despite alliances or adversity. It is everyday actions we take to reach our unexpected or pre-determined goals."

—CB Bowman

Many people talk about courage, but only some know how to identify and implement it daily! And even more, people confuse resilience with courage. This confusion is because courage can mean something different to us —courage is in the eye of the beholder©. Let's start the discussion by considering the following definition of resilience:

Resilience Is the ability to withstand adversity and bounce back from complex life events. Being resilient is being able to withstand or recover quickly from difficult conditions.

The research of Dr. Brené Brown has revealed a difference between resilience and courage. "Courage requires a level of vulnerability and willingness to be open with other people who can support you. By contrast, resilience often hides behind a façade of strength; the stress it creates can harm relationships at work and home."

In the workplace, we often face situations where we have to make difficult decisions. If we are not resilient, it may be easy for us to get frustrated and give up on our goals. That's where courage comes in.

"Courage is about overcoming failure and having the strength to keep going," explained Dr. Amy Cuddy, a Harvard Business School Professor and author of *Presence: Bringing Your Boldest Self to Your Biggest Challenges*. It is also about the ability to expand *success and nurture and grow your success*. The ability to do something which deeply concerns us is a force that releases us from paralysis. When combining courage with knowledge and experience, you can move forward quickly; it gives us the power to accept all outcomes, hold on despite challenges, and take risks while continuing to self-motivate. **It offers us unlimited choices.**

We live in a world filled with fear. People are afraid of change. They are scared to try something new. They are so scared to make a mistake and be criticized for it. They are afraid to fail and lose their job, their income, or status. They are afraid to look foolish. They are afraid to be seen as fearful! This book aims to empower you to take action *despite* your fears. Let this book influence you to have courage by giving up self-imposed blocks by standing up, speaking up, standing tall, and being bold.

Courage to Lead & Lead is an inspiring book that helps individuals take their organization and personal life to the next level with practical advice and lessons. It is based on real-life stories of transformation, failure, success, and courage. In both business and life, by using Microcourage©, you can transform your perceptions and beliefs and make a *seismic* shift in outcomes. Courage is the quality that allows us to act in new ways beyond our self-imposed limitations.

This book includes a roadmap designed to help everyone adopt new ways of thinking and behaving by adapting Microcourage© as the framework for creating change. If you think courage is only for the battlefield or sports arena, think again. The Courage to Lead and Leap will show you how to identify the six behaviors associated with courage and provide you with the tools needed to stand out in a competitive world.

In the behaviors section starts, I start with a famous and inspirational quote then I present true reflective stories of Microcourage© I experienced myself. **As a master storyteller, my goal is for this book to give you the confidence to have the courage to leap & lead through tears and laughter.**

Microcourage© Behaviors

*"I went into the woods because I wished to live deliber-
ately, to front only the essential facts of life, and see if
I could not learn, what it had to teach, and not, when I
came to die, discover that I had not lived."*

—Henry David Thoreau

Six **behaviors are used to define courage. They include
physical, social, moral, emotional, intellectual, and
spiritual.**

I used my life to provide an example for each behavior. By
exploring each behavior with her through her stories, being
courageous will seem more relatable. Her challenge for you is
to replace her story with your own on the provided journaling
pages. Then, when times become challenging, you can look back
on your pages for encouragement to move forward. Some of her
stories are related to business, and some relate to life in general.
Some are funny, some are sad, and some are romantic. However,
all will offer lessons learned if you let them.

Physical Behavior

Physical behavior is the ability to do what is right, regardless of
anxiety or concern. It includes the willingness to say "no" even
when it may be politically incorrect. It is a resolve to stand up for

yourself or others even when doing so may go against cultural norms. It's about being willing to take that first step when unsure where it will lead.

Physical courage at work is the ability to do what is right, regardless of imminent risk, such as being terminated, shunned by your colleagues, or adverse political or social consequences. It may be a resolve simply to make a difference within your office community. These are defined by one's personal beliefs and values, thus requiring an aerial understanding of oneself and those around you.

Surprisingly, physical behavior relates to implementing courage through how we carry ourselves. Our posture, body language, and facial expressions can convey a sense of confidence and assertiveness, which are essential components of courage. For example, standing up straight, making eye contact, and using a firm voice can signal to others that we are self-assured and capable, even in challenging situations. Conversely, slouching, avoiding eye contact, and speaking timidly or uncertainly can make us appear vulnerable and undermine our sense of courage.

Moreover, physical behavior can help us regulate our emotions and manage fear, which is critical for implementing courage. When we encounter situations that trigger worry or anxiety, our body's natural response is to activate the sympathetic nervous system, which prepares us for fight or flight. This can cause physical symptoms such as increased heart rate, rapid breathing, and tense muscles, making it difficult to think clearly or act decisively. However, we can counteract these symptoms and maintain our composure by engaging in physical behaviors that promote relaxation and calmness.

One effective physical behavior for managing fear and anxiety is deep breathing. By taking slow, deep breaths from the diaphragm, we can activate the parasympathetic nervous system, which helps slow down our heart rate, reduce muscle tension, and promote relaxation. This exercise can be beneficial in high-stress situations where we must remain calm and focused, such as giving a speech, confronting a difficult person, or performing in a high-pressure environment. In addition, by practicing deep breathing regularly, we can train our bodies to respond more effectively to stress and increase our capacity for courage.

Another physical behavior that can support courage is exercise. Regular physical activity has been shown to reduce stress, anxiety, and depression while also improving mood, cognitive function, and overall health. By engaging in exercise, we can increase our physical fitness and resilience, which can help us cope better with the physical demands of challenging situations. Moreover, practice can provide a sense of accomplishment and confidence, translating into more extraordinary courage and assertiveness in other areas of our lives.

Finally, physical behavior can also be a powerful tool for expressing courage and standing up for our beliefs and values. When we face opposition or resistance to our ideas or actions, physical behaviors such as standing firm, maintaining eye contact, and using a solid and assertive tone of voice can signal our determination and commitment to our beliefs. In addition, by using physical behaviors that demonstrate courage and conviction, we can inspire others to follow our lead and create positive change.

Concisely, physical behavior plays a critical role in implementing courage. By regulating our emotions, managing fear and anxiety, and expressing confidence and assertiveness, we can develop the physical skills and attributes necessary for courageous action. Through practices such as deep breathing, exercise, and body language, we can train our bodies to respond effectively to stress and adversity while demonstrating the courage that inspires others to follow our lead. While courage may be primarily a mental and emotional trait, physical behavior is an essential component of its implementation and can help us to overcome our fears and achieve our goals in life.

Social Behavior

Social courage is about the self-confidence to engage with others even when unsure of the outcome. It's about standing up for your ideas and being true to yourself. It can simply be the courage to lead an organization, a group, or an individual without knowing the outcome, especially in the face of fear and anxiety.

Social courage at work could be related to speaking up about a wrong or a right, or it could relate to introducing a new product, procedure, or service. It could even be related to whistleblowing or asking for a raise! In his work, author Daniel Goleman defines social courage as: "The ability to act with poise, confidence and composure in tense situations."

Moral Behavior

Essentially, moral courage refers to a person's conviction and bravery in acting in the face of their beliefs or interests. Using, for example, moral courage in the workplace can be an intimidating environment for anyone, especially when you're partaking in a new endeavor or standing up for your rights, the rights of others, beliefs, or values. Moral courage is a difficult quality in the workplace for fear of severe retribution, which can affect your livelihood forever. Several challenges may seem impossible at first – but with moral courage and perseverance, people can support themselves and others struggling with something meaningful.

Being faced with adversity and risk doing the "Right Thing" may mean standing up for an idea or values, exposing an unsafe situation, taking action to correct wrongdoings, or protecting someone else from harm. It involves acting morally even when it isn't easy, popular, or convenient. It's about standing up for the greater good and putting your interests aside for others. There are times when we have to stand up and do something unpopular. Taking a leap of faith and demonstrating this behavior is essential in business and life to ensure growth and stimulate innovation. In summary, it is the ability to act according to personal beliefs, despite fear of consequences or pressure from others.

It is essential to recognize that there are many different types of courage and that moral courage is one of the most important. Moral courage involves standing up for what is right even when doing so may put oneself at risk, whether that risk is physical, emotional, or social.

Implementing courage requires people to act on their moral beliefs even when they are not widespread, go against the status quo, or challenge authority. It is important to note that implementing courage does not always involve taking a physical risk or putting oneself in harm's way. It can also include speaking up in a difficult conversation or making a difficult decision that may negatively affect oneself or others.

One example of this behavior that requires courage is when a person witnesses' injustice and decides to speak out against it. It can be challenging because the person may face retaliation or backlash from those benefiting from the unjust situation. Nevertheless, it takes courage to stand up to those who hold power, challenge their beliefs, and put oneself at risk for the sake of justice.

Another example of moral behavior requiring courage is when someone decides to speak out against something they believe is wrong, even if it goes against the prevailing social norms. It could be speaking out against discrimination or bigotry, challenging the status quo in some way, or advocating for a cause that is not popular. It takes courage to stand up for what one believes in, even when it is not easy or popular.

Courage can also be seen in the decisions we make in our daily lives. For example, it takes courage to admit when we have made a mistake, to apologize to someone we have wronged, or to make amends for past behavior. These acts of courage require us to put our egos aside, acknowledge our mistakes, and take responsibility for our actions.

Moral behavior and courage are closely related because both require a strong sense of ethics and values. When we act morally, we work by our beliefs about right and wrong. It means we clearly understand our values and principles and are willing to act on them even when difficult or uncomfortable. Similarly, courage requires a strong sense of ethics and importance because it requires us to work following our beliefs, even when risky or unpopular.

The relationship between moral behavior and courage is only sometimes straightforward, however. Sometimes, acting morally may require us to exercise caution or avoid risks that could put ourselves or others in danger. For example, it may be ethically correct to speak out against injustice, but doing so in a way that puts oneself at risk may not be the best course of action. In these situations, it takes courage to follow one's values without putting oneself or others in harm's way.

The relationship between moral behavior and courage is a complex one. Both concepts require a strong sense of ethics and values, and both need us to act by following those beliefs, even when it is difficult or unpopular. But on the other hand, implementing courage requires us to work on our moral convictions, stand up for what is right even when it is risky or uncomfortable, and to take responsibility for our actions.

Emotional Behavior

It is expressing your feelings and needs while taking responsibility for your senses. How often have you read about an industry titan suffering or who has been diagnosed with a mental or physical ailment? Or worse yet, committed suicide. Many popular business books for our leaders tackle the subject of emotional courage, including self-awareness and self-management skills.

From the top global executive coach Marshall Goldsmith's book, we have *Triggers: Creating Behavior That Lasts--Becoming the Person You Want to Be.* From Marcella Allison's book, *Why Didn't Anybody Tell Me This Sh*t Before? Wit and Wisdom from Women in Business*, the list is endless. However, at the core, we must ask ourselves, do our leaders have the moxie to incorporate behaviors related to emotional courage in the workplace? We have to examine whether or not our leaders have the ability and the capacity to acknowledge and respond *appropriately* to one's own emotions and those of others.

While the two examples in this book relate to personal emotions, the philosophy is the same in the workplace. Emotional courage is a behavior we have seen very little of in our leaders in Corporate America. This is especially true before COVID-19 and the other four pandemics (Social Justice, Environment, Economics, and Mental Health) we are simultaneously experiencing. It is a behavior that our leaders shun as having no place in our workplace.

Even our laws make it difficult to express emotion. For example, a leader/manager cannot ask employees why they requested sick leave or how they were doing due to being out sick. These questions are considered a violation of privacy and prohibited due to laws like HIPAA (The Health Insurance Portability and Accountability Act of 1996) and the Security and Breach Notification Rules. HIPAA is a federal law requiring national standards to protect sensitive patient health information from being disclosed without the patient's consent or knowledge and other such compliance rules.

Looking back, we must ask ourselves if this indifferent or apathetic behavior has served leaders well in dealing with employee mental health. We must also ask if we are mentally prepared for the next big crisis or pandemic.

Do our leaders have the capacity to display emotional behavior when it involves the boardroom, the public, or employees?

Emotional behavior and courage are closely related and two essential aspects that significantly shape an individual's personality. Emotional behavior refers to how individuals respond to different situations, while courage refers to the ability to face and overcome fears and challenges. Implementing courage requires an individual to understand and regulate their emotions.

A crucial role in implementing courage is emotional behavior because emotions are the driving force behind actions. Fear, anxiety, and uncertainty can hold individuals from taking risks and facing challenges. Courageous individuals are not free from fear or anxiety but have learned to manage their emotions and act despite their fears.

One of the primary emotions that prevent individuals from implementing courage is fear. Fear is a natural response to danger but can also hold individuals back from taking risks and facing challenges. Individuals who lack emotional regulation skills tend to be overwhelmed by their fears and may avoid situations they perceive as dangerous. For instance, a person may be afraid of public speaking and may avoid speaking in general due to the fear of embarrassment. However, the courageous individual understands that fear is a normal emotion and learns to manage their fear through emotional regulation. Courageous individuals can face their fears and take action.

Another emotion that is closely related to courage is anxiety. Anxiety is a feeling of worry, unease, or nervousness that individuals experience in response to stress or uncertainty. It is interesting that anxiety can prevent individuals from taking risks and facing challenges but can also motivate them to act. For example, an individual may feel anxious about an upcoming job interview, but the anxiety may inspire them to prepare thoroughly. Emotional regulation is essential in managing anxiety because it helps individuals to identify the source of their anxiety and develop strategies to manage it. By managing their anxiety, individuals can implement courage and take action despite their fears.

Self-doubt is another emotion that can prevent individuals from implementing courage. Self-doubt is the feeling of uncertainty about one's abilities or decisions. Self-doubt can lead to indecision and inaction but it can also motivate individuals to work harder and achieve their goals. Emotional regulation is crucial in managing self-doubt because it helps individuals to identify the source of their doubts and develop strategies to overcome them. For example, an individual who doubts their ability to complete a project may break down the project into smaller tasks and focus on completing each to build their confidence. By managing their self-doubt, individuals can implement courage and take action to achieve their goals.

Emotional behavior is also related to courage in terms of resilience. Resilience is the ability to recover from setbacks, challenges, and adversity. Individuals who lack emotional regulation skills may become overwhelmed by setbacks and give up on their goals. However, courageous individuals are resilient and can bounce back from setbacks and challenges. Emotional regulation helps individuals to develop resilience by teaching them to manage their emotions and focus on solutions rather than problems. By developing resilience, individuals can implement courage and continue to pursue their goals despite setbacks and challenges.

Finally, emotional behavior is related to courage in terms of empathy. Empathy is the ability to understand and share the feelings of others. Courageous individuals are empathetic and understand that their actions can impact others. Emotional regulation helps individuals to develop empathy by teaching them to understand their own emotions and the emotions of others. By developing empathy, individuals can implement courage in a way that is considerate of others and their feelings.

In conclusion, emotional behavior is closely related to implementing courage because emotions drive actions. Emotional regulation is vital.

Intellectual Behavior

A leader who uses intellectual behavior means they dare to make hard decisions, accept calculated risks, and innovate ahead of the competition.

This also means having the ability and capacity (the ability to use and understand information to make a decision and communicate any decision made) to speak one's mind in a way that allows others to affirm or reject what they say. Finally, it is knowing themselves, being honest, and expressing ideas freely.

Leaders who display intellectual behavior speak unpopular truths, challenge conventional wisdom and make brave decisions. It's not only about being willing to embrace innovation and accept calculated risks, but it also involves putting others before themself for the greater good. They tend to use and encourage others to use simple strategies and techniques to increase confidence; self-awareness; resilience, and perseverance through self-reflection; community engagement, and connecting with new role models from all sectors of the economy. This development aide results in increasing intellectual bench strength.

Intellectual courage allows leaders to work with customers and partners to solve complex challenges and address their business needs

This type of courage with rigorous empirical evidence, along with scientific, technical, and design processes; allows these leaders to come up often coming up with solutions not afforded by others.

In the workplace, this may mean challenging the higher-level C-suite, advocating for employees, or implementing new processes that may result in losing workers. The decision to take risks is a courageous and noble one. However, the courage to lead and innovate requires perseverance and vision identified through intellectual behavior.

Intellectual behavior is a crucial aspect of our cognitive abilities, as it involves using rational and analytical thinking to solve problems, make decisions, and assess situations. Implementing courage, on the other hand, consists in taking bold and risky actions despite the potential consequences or fears involved. At first glance, these two concepts may seem unrelated, but upon closer examination, it becomes clear that intellectual behavior is essential for implementing courage.

One way in which intellectual behavior relates to implementing courage is through critical thinking. Critical thinking involves analyzing and evaluating information, arguments, and evidence to arrive at a well-reasoned conclusion. When faced with a challenging or risky situation, individuals who engage in critical thinking are better equipped to make informed decisions that balance the potential benefits and risks. By taking a step back and examining the situation from various angles, they can identify potential pitfalls and devise strategies to overcome them, thereby reducing the fear of failure or negative consequences. For example, a business owner considering expanding their operations into a new market might use critical thinking to assess the risks and benefits of this decision, analyzing market trends, competition, and potential customer demand. By doing so, they can make a well-informed decision that requires courage but is less likely to fail.

Another way in which intellectual behavior relates to implementing courage is through creativity. Creative thinking involves generating new ideas, approaches, or solutions to overcome obstacles or challenges. When faced with a risky or daunting task, individuals who engage in creative thinking can develop innovative strategies that reduce the fear of failure or negative consequences. In addition, by exploring unconventional or out-of-the-box ideas, they can find solutions that others may not have considered, giving them an edge in achieving their goals.

For example, an artist struggling to find inspiration might use creative thinking to explore new mediums, techniques, or subject matter, ultimately producing bold and innovative work that requires courage to share with the world.

Furthermore, intellectual behavior relates to implementing courage through resilience. Resilience involves:

- Recovering from setbacks or failures.
- Learning from them.
- Moving forward with renewed determination.

When faced with a challenging or risky situation, individuals who engage in resilient thinking can bounce back from setbacks, using them as learning opportunities to strengthen their resolve and motivation. By adopting a growth mindset that sees failure as a temporary setback rather than a permanent obstacle, they can persevere through challenges requiring courage. For example, an athlete who has suffered a severe injury might use resilient thinking to recover, rehabilitate, and return to their sport with renewed determination and courage.

Finally, intellectual behavior relates to implementing courage through self-awareness. Self-awareness involves understanding one's thoughts, feelings, behaviors and how they affect others. When faced with a risky or challenging situation, individuals who engage in self-aware thinking can assess their strengths and weaknesses, fears and motivations, and adjust their approach accordingly. By understanding their limitations and tendencies, they can devise strategies that match their strengths and mitigate their weaknesses, reducing the fear of failure or negative consequences. For example, a public speaker nervous about giving a presentation might use self-aware thinking to identify their strengths, such as their knowledge of the topic, and weaknesses, such as their tendency to speak too quickly. Then, by adjusting their pace and emphasizing their expertise, they can give a successful presentation that requires courage.

Intellectual behavior is essential for implementing courage, providing the tools and mindset necessary to overcome obstacles and take bold actions. By engaging in critical thinking, resilience, and self-awareness, individuals can make informed decisions, find innovative solutions, recover from setbacks, and understand their strengths and weaknesses. By doing so, they can build the courage necessary to take on challenges.

Spiritual Behavior

Generally speaking, this refers to the art of leadership in the business world. A spiritual leader emerges when they dare to align with their values, beliefs, and morals —even when doing so may be difficult or unpopular. It's a willingness to build consensus, seek win-win solutions, and collaborate across teams. When teams collaborate, they achieve more. Collaboration can be challenging in any setting but is especially hard in times of crisis.

This leadership behavior is seen in people who inspire us to identify and use new ways of thinking and to be together. It encourages new methods, which are more expansive than anything we could have imagined without added input. They show us how powerful it is to empower others than to wield power over them. They teach us to stand up for values despite a crisis, empowering everyone to succeed.

As leaders, we must lead and inspire others. The more people are empowered and inspired, the more powerful they become. We can only achieve greatness by working collaboratively with others and acting in alignment with our values, beliefs, and morals.

By spiritual behavior in the workplace, we are not necessarily talking about religion; this is not to say that it can't be included.

For example, by opening our courage muscle and experiencing a colleague's religious convictions, we can build a stronger bond that can strengthen our Microcourage©. *"Microcourage© is built on a foundation of knowledge."*

Spirituality is often associated with an individual's life quest for meaning and purpose. It involves connecting with a higher power, whether God, the universe, or one's inner self, and living by spiritual principles. One such principle is courage, which can be defined as the ability to face fear and take action in the face of it.

At its core, spiritual behavior is about living in alignment with one's values and beliefs. It can include practicing gratitude, forgiveness, kindness, and compassion towards oneself and others. These behaviors require courage, as they often involve facing uncomfortable emotions and challenging situations.

For example, forgiveness requires the courage to let go of anger and resentment towards those who have wronged us. It involves acknowledging our pain and releasing it rather than holding onto it. This takes considerable courage because it can be challenging to face the hurt someone else has caused and let go of the desire for revenge or justice.

Similarly, practicing kindness and compassion towards others requires the courage to be vulnerable and open-hearted. It involves recognizing our shared humanity and extending empathy and love even when it may not be reciprocated. Again, this takes courage because it requires us to let go of our ego and trust in the inherent goodness of others.

In addition to these individual behaviors, spiritual behavior can involve working toward more significant societal and environmental issues. It can include advocating for social justice, protecting the environment, and promoting peace. These efforts require courage because they often involve challenging the status quo and speaking out against injustice.

For example, advocating for social justice may involve speaking out against racism, sexism, and other forms of discrimination. It requires the courage to confront systemic inequalities and to push for change, even when it may be met with resistance.

Protecting the environment requires courage, as it often involves standing up to powerful industries and advocating for sustainable practices. In addition, it can mean challenging consumer culture, choosing a more eco-conscious lifestyle, or advocating for policies prioritizing environmental protection over economic growth.

Finally, promoting peace and nonviolence requires a great deal of courage. It involves responding to conflict with compassion and empathy rather than violence or aggression. It takes courage because it requires us to overcome our instincts for self-protection and to trust in the power of love and connection.

Overall, spiritual behavior is intimately connected to the implementation of courage. By living in alignment with our values and beliefs, we can cultivate the courage to face fear and take action in its face. These can involve individual practices such as forgiveness, compassion, and greater societal and environmental efforts toward justice and peace.

In addition to its relationship to courage, spiritual behavior can provide strength and resilience in the face of adversity. By connecting with a higher power and living in alignment with spiritual principles, individuals can tap into a more profound sense of purpose and meaning in life. In addition, it can provide a sense of grounding and resilience in difficult situations.

For example, individuals who practice meditation and mindfulness may find they can better cope with stress and anxiety. They can approach difficult emotions with greater equanimity and self-compassion by cultivating a sense of present-moment awareness and non-judgmental acceptance.

Similarly, individuals with a strong sense of faith or spirituality may find they can better cope with illness or loss. By trusting in a higher power and finding meaning in difficult circumstances, they can find hope and resilience that helps them persevere through challenging times.

Spiritual behavior is intimately connected to the implementation of courage. By living in alignment with our values and beliefs, we can cultivate the courage to face fear and take action in the face. Whether through individual practices such as forgiveness and compassion or more significant societal efforts towards justice and peace, spiritual behavior requires us to be brave and face discomfort head-on. Moreover, this behavior can provide a sense of strength and resilience in the face of adversity. By connecting with a higher power and finding meaning in difficult situations, individuals can tap into a more profound sense of purpose and hope that helps them persevere through challenging times.

It's important to note, however, that spiritual behavior and courage are not guaranteed against life challenges or difficulties. Even the most devout spiritual practitioners can face adversity and struggle with fear and uncertainty. However, by living in alignment with spiritual principles and cultivating the courage to face discomfort, we can build resilience and a sense of purpose that helps us to navigate life's challenges with greater ease.

The relationship between spiritual behavior and courage is powerful. By living in alignment with our values and beliefs, we can cultivate the courage to face fear and take action in the face of it. Whether through individual practices or more considerable societal efforts, spiritual behavior requires us to be brave and face discomfort head-on. **Through this process, we can build resilience and find a sense of purpose that helps us navigate life's challenges more easily.**

My Journeys of Microcourage© Behavior

Physical Behavior

Story: But I Was Hungry!

*"Strength does not come from physical capacity.
It comes from an indomitable will."*

—Mahatma Gandhi

I was traveling from England to France by boat in the coach section, and I remember when the ship ran out of sandwiches. However, the first class still had sandwiches, and I was hungry, so I decided to take a risk and order a sandwich in first class. Sitting at the bar, I overheard a conversation between the waiter and an American woman. The customer was quite angry because she was trying to order food in English, and the steward, a Frenchman, proclaimed that he did not speak English. I remember her distinct cat-eye sunglasses and her look of utter disgust. She was fuming.

Sitting between us was a young Belgian man whom I looked at in absolute shame about the woman's behavior as a fellow American. This woman was displaying such poor behavior that I thought if the waiter didn't serve her, I would not stand a chance of being served as a black American. So, I turned to the young

Belgian man, who had earlier introduced himself as Lewis, and asked, "comment dit-on sandwich en français, s'il vous plait » (how do you say sandwich in French, please)?

I did not realize that the waiter heard me; he came over and said, "for you, young lady, I will speak English." I looked at him, surprised and confused; as he walked away, I said to Lewis, "I thought he didn't speak English." Lewis replied, "all stewards on this crossing must speak at least five languages, English, French, German, Italian, and Spanish." I gasped in shock. I then understood that the steward chose not to help the other American woman, given she had not respectfully attempted to try to speak the language of his country.

From this small act of having the courage to speak up and ask a stranger about the language of the waiter's mother country and, quite frankly, utter hunger, I learned it doesn't take a lot to embrace and respect a different culture so that *you* are equally welcomed and respected.

For many years following this encounter, Lewis and I remained close friends. I had the opportunity to have several memorable trips to Belgium at the invitation of Lewis and his family. Some memories were sad; one morning, I woke up to hear the news that Arthur Ashe, the celebrated black tennis player, had died of AIDS due to a blood transfusion. Some were fascinating, like the many stories of how Lewis's father learned to speak English during the war by listening to the radio. Lewis's mom taught me how to cook Belgium dishes like Waterzooi de Poisson (a fish stew), and I enjoyed Belgium waffles and Moules served with fries. While walking down the streets of Belgium, I enjoyed eating fries with mayonnaise for the first time, and let's not forget the famous Belgium chocolates. **These are memories and lessons I will cherish forever.**

Journal of Microcourage©

Write Your Physical Behavior Story:

_____

_____

_____

_____

_____

_____

_____

_____

_____

_____

_____

_____

_____

_____

_____

_____

_____

_____

_____

_____

Social Courage Behavior

Story: What the F–k!

"My America, Where Has She Gone"
My heart has been ripped apart
My ambition has been ripped from my hands
My dreams have been poisoned
My America, where has she gone?
My America, was she ever here?
My America is not your America
My youth was filled with dreams of success
My bank would be filled to the rim
My hand would reach out to others
My America, where has she gone?
My friends they disappeared,
as the light of Corporate America loomed with gloom
My heart sank with reality
Where was the space for me to shine?
My brain said let me out, my brain said feed me!
My America, where has she gone?
The story is still unfinished
Floyd has spoken from his grave
Let me rise as Jesus once did
My America, where has she gone?
Floyd in his passing said, let me return America
to all who heard me scream in the agony and pain
of my death, give America to all!
My America, where has she gone?
I see her in my dreams
I see her in my heart
I see her in my tears
My America, where has she gone?"

Was it courage, tenacity, or anger? Was it shock, resilience, or disappointment? A combination of everything. I don't know. I am glad I responded as I did. I'm elated that I fought back in a way I knew I'd be proud of, a way that would benefit me both in the immediate and long run. I knew I needed to improve my self-confidence, and I wanted to be proud of my work and contributions to my company. I did not know the physical and mental toll it would take on me then and in the future.

I was working for a Fortune 500 company where I experienced incredible racism, but I was naive, and it was subtle. It was so delicate and precise that it was difficult to analyze or describe. As a result, I thought that was just how it was for many years and ignored the treatment I received. However, sadly this contributed to what I thought must have been my paranoia. Having had no corporate experience and not having knowledge of "Corporate speak," I was behind the eight ball. I worked hard, nose to the grind, long and productive hours. I was so proud of my work, yet I secretly feared how good I was. I know that it does not make sense. But I feared others would scorn me, yet I could not figure out where that fear came from. I now realize I was dealing with a combination of racism and being bullied. I was bullied and belittled for my talents, just enough to make me feel "less than others."

With the help of an attorney, now a close friend, I had my eyes and awareness open to disrespectful conversations, non-recognition, being assigned low-profile projects, identifying weak spots for me that were considered strengths in others, impossible deadlines, and the excuses which were provided for lack of promotions. One of the most egregious experiences was when my manager drew pygmies and passed them around when I refused to purchase lunch for her. In addition, vendors who were management friends were encouraged to offer me bribes, otherwise known as entrapment opportunities.

At the time, I was working in marketing for ready-to-eat products – known today as "branding." I was responsible for bringing the marketing department's concepts to life. Consumers couldn't taste what was in the package; it was up to me to create enough visual appeal on the package to positively influence their buying decision. The box had to communicate nutrition, health, taste, fun, and something new worth trying. In addition, consumers had to feel they were purchasing an *experience,* an experience that would outweigh the competition in a sea of other-like products in the store.

One particular product represented a breakthrough in the industry for the product itself and the packaging. We had not delved into this type of product or product presentation before, but we had no choice. Our competition was kicking our ass with products in this space. A lot was riding on the package design and the product. Focus groups helped provide valuable feedback on the product; however, we only received praise about the packaging. As a result, management still had a significant concern regarding the design. We had to create new tooling to produce the product, which was a substantial investment for the company, and our printers were wondering if they could create quality graphics for the wrapping; we were also running out of launch time. We continued to send the box design and the product through focus groups. Given that the design represented an industry breakthrough in the market, I had to have the courage to fight for the design while my marketing client fought for the product.

Finally, the decision was made to roll out the new product in the new package design in additional test markets. Again, the test market results were the highest praise for our existing service and product launches.

For the large part, consumers purchase based on what they see —the packaging plays a significant role in the purchasing decision (especially for new products). So, after the focus groups, we knew we had a hit the product, but the big question was whether a consumer would pick up the product within three seconds of seeing it on the shelf based on the package design.

Yes, you read that right! *Three seconds* was all we had to attract the consumer —three seconds to catch the buyer's eye among rows and rows of other products.

I was so proud when the test results returned as having hit the bullseye for the design. It was so successful that the box design received two prestigious awards. I was excited to receive the letter saying that the packaging design had won both awards; for one, the ceremony was in Italy, and I was invited to accept the award.

I could not wait to tell the department head. Much to my shock, I received a lackluster response. The department head told me the trip would have to receive approval from a higher-level manager *and the legal department.*

Weeks later, I received a shocking response.

I would not be able to accept the award. The reason? The organization didn't see the value in it. Instead, they suggested I should consider sending someone from the printing company to accept the award. I was devastated, I was angry, I was hurt, I was confused. I even felt ashamed that I had asked in the first place.

The only thing I knew was that I would have the courage to go against the decision; I would go to Italy to accept that award. I had to have the courage to challenge the system.

I thought about it for a long time. *How could I make this trip?* Then the answer came: I would use my vacation time and pay for the trip myself! Thank goodness I had banked my vacation days and had the time to go. Next was figuring out the expenses. Finally, I decided to use my savings to take the trip. The company tried to argue that I could not use my saved vacation days simultaneously! Fortunately, the employee handbook demolished that roadblock.

The trip to Italy was one of the most rewarding experiences of my life. Standing on stage and accepting the award using an Italian translator made me almost forget the horrors of the responses I received from my company and the fear of going to a foreign country to give a speech and accept an award. The incredible experience of traveling to another country and being welcomed with open arms was one I will never forget. I gained motivation and inspiration from the trip; to create even better containers after seeing the designs from another country. I remember this was the first time I had ever seen a Tetra Pak, which uses aseptic packaging technology.

It was a mind-boggling experience that stimulated and increased creativity in my mind. And let's not forget to mention the food, the culture, the arts, and the people, all of which added to an extraordinary adventure and the strengthening of my courage, knowing that I had made the correct decision *to speak up, stand up, stand out and be bold.*

The knowledge that I dared to do the right thing for me was incredibly satisfying; this is something I did for myself, allowing me to see my strength, courage, and resolve. I did not focus on the rejection from the company I worked for; I only focused on the positives of experiencing a fantastic new and thrilling experience. I focused on my Microcourage©.

Little did I know at the time that many, many years later, this would become only part of my story because it didn't stop there **—I ended up marrying an Italian man!**

Journal of Microcourage©

Write Your Social Behavior Story:

_____

_____

_____

_____

_____

_____

_____

_____

_____

_____

_____

_____

_____

_____

_____

_____

_____

_____

_____

Moral Courage Behavior

Story #1: I Watched Them Kill Him

"I've learned that people will forget what you said, people will forget what you did, but people will never forget how you made them feel."

—Maya Angelou

I remember immediately following the killing of George Floyd, staying up one night to watch The Tonight Show with Jimmy Fallon. While interviewing a female actress, he asked her what she thought about the killing of George Floyd and the aftermath. She responded, I don't think it's my responsibility to teach white people how to behave or respect black people. So, I thought, *right on, sister*, and then fell asleep.

The following day, I woke up, and I thought about the show and my reaction, and then something happened. Several thoughts came flooding into my head --- I thought of John F. Kennedy, and I thought of Martin Luther King Jr. and Malcolm X, and I said to myself, *If not me, then who? Who will teach white people? How can one learn without dialogue, without someone to learn from, without someone to ask what some would consider ignorant questions?*

My memory returned to my days of sadness and horror, ultimately resulting in my taking legal action against two Fortune 500 companies for race discrimination. I remember the sickening feeling each day I had to get up and go to work for these companies while taking legal actions. I remembered the courage it took; I remembered being shunned by my black *and* white colleagues. People walked in the other direction when they saw me coming down the halls. It also triggered thoughts of my working at organizations where discrimination was so prevalent that I had become exhausted from fighting back; still, I mustered up the strength and courage to continue the fight for myself and for others to follow in my path.

I was not counting on my courage leaving me spent, so I had to take time off from the struggle to regain my strength and sanity. My fight left me sad and *empty but with respect for my actions* which remained dormant until the killing of George Floyd.

However, the reality was that this courage had served me for many years and would continue to do so for many more years. I developed untold strength, resolve, and a keen eye to know when wrong was done to me or others. I also gained the ability to fight back with sharp smarts. I learned the importance of building credibility and building what I call "listening language" (the art of gaining and holding someone's attention and resulting in a positive action) necessary for being an influencer.

With the killing of George Floyd, an old part of me resurged and merged with the new me; I remembered thinking, *CB, it's time to have the courage to stand up and speak out again!* You have unmasked credibility in the field of Courage and Corporate Executive Coaching. You are a person who can speak out. And you are a person who can listen. You must have the courage to join the voices of others in support of social justice.

In the days pursuing this revolution, I received a call from a CEO asking for help with what to do as a leader in his organization following the killing of Floyd. For several weeks I coached him using my "no blame, no shame" approach. He was incredibly grateful as he began to see things in a different light regarding racism and how to respond courageously as a heartfelt leader.

I decided to open a company named "Workplace Equality and Equity" (WEE). It was based on a "no shame, no blame" approach to resolving the issues of racism in corporate America. I identified a board of advisors and a team of thought-leader facilitators to pull together learning laboratories. This concept took courage for me to step out and the courage for me to step up.

It took months for us to pull together a best-in-class program for helping organizations solve the issue of racism within their walls. As a team, we felt excellent about what we'd built. It took us a year before we were ready with a complete program and a conference.

Sadly, time had passed, and the public had waned on its interest in social justice and the killing of Floyd; they were onto the next big hairy elephant in the room: mental health. Floyd had become a "cry" of the past! Mental health has become a new crisis for organizations. We never picked up the expected speed, especially with all the competitors in the arena before us. The competitors presented the same rhetoric as before —nothing sustainable —but it made organizations feel good until calm was regained. For people of color, there is no real expectation for resolving racism; there is only hope. Sadly, **bandages work until the mind forgets.**

"Having courage does not always result in the success as we think it should."

—CB Bowman

The courage to move forward and design a program that could help many people did not sell; however, it brought together a group of leaders to discuss, share, and resolve. The leaders who participated in creating the program were a diverse population. We had a chance to hear and feel what was in our hearts and minds. We had an extraordinary experience of courage shared as one.

Am I thrilled that I took the step to bring together great minds, sharing and resolving? YES! Am I sad that it did not have wings? YES!

We had the opportunity to hear from the LBGTQ community; we had the chance to hear from the Asian community about the experience of Asian hate; we had a chance to hear from a man in Africa about racism in South Africa and why he felt so strongly that his country experienced racism on a different level than America; we had a chance to experience a black female whose daughter's boyfriend had just been murdered; we had an opportunity to experience a black female who was living in the south and dating a white male; and we had a chance to hear from a privileged white female about her experience.

Courage has given me an extraordinary opportunity to listen, learn, share, and experience the world of others through their lens. It allowed me to share my world without blame, shame, or fear of retribution. If only everyone could have the courage to have the richness of that experience. **Imagine the possibilities**.

Moral Courage Behavior

Story #2: "Shut Up, Madam CEO"

"Ubuntu"

The word Ubuntu is derived from an old folk saying "Umuntu ngumuntu ngabantu" which literally translates to "A person is a person, because of other people."

"Sawu Bona"
Is from the Ubuntu Culture of South Africa.
Literally translated, this word means "I See You"

One day, during an Executive Advisory Committee meeting for my company, the Association of Corporate Executive Coaches, I asked if anyone had anything to add after giving what I thought was a meaty presentation on the state of affairs. There was silence for two very long minutes.

One member finally spoke up. "CB, what is our role in these meetings?" I was puzzled. "It has not changed since we started meeting three years ago," I said. "It is to offer advice, and add value to the organization's growth."

At which point, *several* more members joined the conversation, and one said, "Well, CB, when will you *allow us* to do our jobs?" I was stunned!

Although I remember them asking me the same question before, I thought I had responded so clearly that I had put the question to rest, but evidently, I had not. There was more to the question than what I was hearing. So, I asked them to elaborate. "Well," one said, "each month, we meet for two hours, and you give us an 'after it has happened' rundown. You never ask us what we think before you do something. How about letting us know what issue you are trying to solve and let us make a recommendation? In addition, allow us the opportunity to offer you alternatives if we disagree?"

"So, you want me to shut up?" I asked. I was met with nervous laughter and a resounding YES!

Again, I was shocked because – in my mind – I had done what they were asking. Quite frankly, I was hurt. This situation was a moral dilemma; it was my company. Who were they to tell me to get out of my way so that the company could grow? Perhaps a better way of saying this is that I was unaware of how self-absorbed I was with my title as the CEO.

Laughingly and sadly, my response was despicable, and I went on strike! I refused to say anything during the meetings. I even went so far as to say, when asked my thoughts to say "Well, you told me that I was getting in the way, so you solved it." Miraculously I had a fantastic Executive Advisory Committee because they recognized my defensiveness was from feeling hurt versus my being sassy. I later realized it was a throwback reaction from my earlier days in corporate America, where racism was rampant, and I was belittled when voicing a thought. Begrudgingly, I had to have the courage to see that the Executive Committee was correct and that was not the same as my experience in Corporate America. As a result of their speaking up, I saw the association grow from 25 people to 100 people quickly! Acknowledging the error of my ways and understanding that recognizing the error of my ways was Microcourage© in action!

About a year later, I watched a live stream broadcast with Dr. Marshall Goldsmith and Alan Mulally. Marshall asked Alan what his greatest lesson was while being the CEO of Ford. He responded, "I learned not to speak first in a meeting because when I do, I learn nothing. People are afraid to speak up after I've spoken, so I would only learn what I was thinking if I spoke first." Laughingly I thought, WOW, I'm in good company learning a valuable lesson!

Remember, *courage is not only speaking up —it is also shutting up when needed!*

Moral Courage Behavior

Story #3: "What Makes You Think You Can
Open a Company!?"

"It always seems impossible until it is done."

—Nelson Mandela

I woke up one morning to bright sunlight on my face and thought, what's next for me? After 20 years of giving my heart, soul, and sweat, this incident occurred after I left a company, only to realize I was a pawn in their discrimination game. I woke up finding myself on the winning side of the legal mumbo jumbo but with no place to call my office, and tears rolled down my face. This morning took place after years of being coached on collecting the correct evidence I needed to prove a case of discrimination while continuing to be a model employee. At one point, I was told by one employment lawyer that he would have to side with my employer because my employer was "the big kahunas."

The tears would not stop as I thought all of "me" no longer existed; yes, I had fought a good fight, I had laid the way for future people of color not to experience the horrors I had gone through, I had called public attention to the new form of slavery... but how did I personally feel? Lost —I thought that the industry would shun me and that I would need to prepare for a new journey at this point, late in my life. I needed courage more than ever before. But I didn't know what I needed courage for—who was I? What was I? Where to next? What training did I have? I thought to myself, think positively! At least I didn't have to worry about paying off my car, mortgage, healthcare insurance, or food in the house. The settlement took care of all of that and more. Most would consider this set for life, but I felt lost.

After wiping away my tears of emptiness, loneliness, and devastation, I thought, OK, time to have the courage to move on, stop the pity session and figure out what was next! What was next came to my mind like a ball of fire. I wanted to use my experience in coaching to help others not have the same painful experience as I had. I wanted to be a full-time career coach.

Fast forward, I became excellent as a coach, and I loved the work but wanted to take it up a level, so I joined an outplacement firm. It had its challenges because there needed to be people of color on the coaching side of the company, and there were none. The reason was that the clients they had were not of color. People of color were hard to find at a level in an organization where they would be granted outplacement services should they be terminated.

The next notch up from an outplacement coach or career coach was to become an executive coach, which I desperately wanted, but the road was once again blocked for people of color. So many years later, I opened the *Association of Corporate Executive Coaches©*, which certifies master-level corporate executive coaches as "Enterprise-wide business partners with their clients©," and I coach senior-level executive coaches on complex client cases.

One day I received a call from a friend who said he was planning on becoming an executive coach. His seemingly odd decision was despite his being the Chief Human Resources Officer (CHRO) who hired corporate executive coaches. He said he would take a program that would grant him certification as an executive coach through an association that was a household name in the coaching space. I wished him luck. About a year later, he called me to say he had a problem getting certified because he needed to be shadowed by someone already approved by the association.

Perplexed, I asked him what the problem was. He said he had interviewed over 25 of their recommended certified coaches to select one, but none knew the meaning of an ROI. He felt that, given his position, it was not a good fit to receive advice from a coach who needed to be more knowledgeable in simple business terminology.

"Let me ask you a question," I said. "If you knew of an association that had corporate executive coaches as its members, who knew what an ROI was and who believed in being "enterprise-wide business partner©, with their clients", would you have gone through this program?" His response was a resounding "no." At this point, I gave birth to the idea of the Association of Corporate Executive Coaches (ACEC). Members would already be trained as executive coaches and who had walked in the shoes of a CXO leader. It had been over 20 years since I started a successful association, and it was in a different field —I needed to do some research.

My research again confirmed a need for an association for executive coaches with a strong business background who could go toe-to-toe with a CEO. *Coaches who believed in being "Enterprise-wide business partners© with their clients."* My instinct told me it needed to be a boutique executive coach association in the United States. I needed to do more research in the field to make this happen. So, one morning, I reached for the phone.

I decided to interview successful, prominent scale association leaders to identify potential points of difference. My goal was not to step on anyone's toes. Instead, I needed to identify a niche I could call my own. So, what was the missing piece(s) that professionals in our field could benefit from in an association?

I contacted two associations in another country, and three here in the United States. One owner brought me to my knees with her response to my query. She emphasized everything *that would go wrong*, what a mistake this was for me to consider this idea, and that there was no need for another association in our field. She also mentioned how good her association was and where she would take it as a next step. She ended by warning me *not* to move forward. The coup de grâce was at the end of the conversation; she said, "I hope I have been able to help you!"

Courage gave me the strength to respond with unambiguous truth!...

"If our conversation was an example of your coaching abilities, I'm afraid our field is in trouble." She apologized profusely, but the damage was done.

My courage led me to build the *Association of Corporate Executive Coaches* (ACEC), which is in its ninth year of success at the time of writing this book.

Journal of Microcourage©

Write Your Moral Behavior Story:

_____

_____

_____

_____

_____

_____

_____

_____

_____

_____

_____

_____

_____

_____

_____

_____

_____

_____

_____

Emotional Courage Behavior

Story #1: I Asked Him to Marry Me

"I learned that courage was not the absence of fear, but the triumph over it. The brave man is not he who does not feel afraid, but he who conquers that fear."

—Nelson Mandela

I remember one day when I was younger, working at a company where I befriended an older colleague. One day I told him, "I'm worried I'll never get married." He said, "CB, you'll get married *when you want to get married!"* I didn't quite understand that response. I had undoubtedly dated and had long-term boyfriends I thought I wanted to marry, and I'd certainly had my share of heartbreaks.

Fast forward many years later, a famous American television host and comedian, Steve Harvey, wrote a book called *Act Like a Lady, Think Like a Man: What Men Really Think About Love, Relationships, Intimacy, and Commitment.* It sounded interesting, so I put aside my business books and devoured every word.

This book was eye-opening for me. Steve Harvey reiterated what I had been told many, many years earlier by my colleague; that it is up to the *woman* to decide when she will get married and to whom. I realized that up to that point, I did not want to get married. WOW. *That* was a mind-blower! However, my tune had changed. I memorized every concept in the book; It became front and center in my mind, and many unrealized fears about getting married surfaced.

Fast forward to 2018 as I sat in my house in New Jersey and decided I was now serious. I called up colleagues, and I said I wanted to get married, and they said you would never find a husband in your line of work —sitting at a computer and being on the phone all of the time! They said you need to get out of the house and your office. OMG, I thought. I'm an introvert, not big on bars, and horrible at parties, and all of my friends were out of the dating scene. The thought terrified me. All of the men I knew were not what I felt were marriageable material. I realized that Steve had skipped —how to *find* the best man to marry, the man with whom you want to invest your time and emotions.

Two colleagues and association members said, "Think of how you can expand your work to meet men. Start thinking positively about ways that you can meet men instead of how you *can't* meet men." In other words, they encouraged me to have the same courage I had already displayed in opening my company.

At this point, I realized how right they were! I hadn't dared to meet a husband! *But what did that mean?* Having the courage to meet —I dated, but it was sobering to realize that I was dating the wrong type for me. As I talked to several friends, I discovered they went online to meet their spouses. I thought that was a waste of time; I'd tried it before, and it never worked. But I suddenly realized that maybe my lack of courage was stopping me from taking the right action to find the right man. I needed to find the courage to be *intentional*. So, I sought their advice on how to find a *good match* online. I even had the courage to ask them to describe me for my ad!

At the same time, I was thinking about finding a husband, and I decided to relocate to Colorado. I knew New Jersey was not going to be the place where I was going to find a soulmate. But the more I researched a new place to live, the more daunting the idea of moving became. Finally, I narrowed the search to three areas, Colorado, Arizona, and New Mexico. Of course, I wanted to visit all three. However, after much research, and the need to have a Costco being only 30 minutes away, at the most, I selected Colorado.

The Microcourage© which came to me took many forms. It included letting go of possessions and putting my paid-off house up for sale in New Jersey while at the same time planning and conducting a conference in California. I don't know whether it was courage or insanity that made me do this. Most people would say it was courage. But I would say it was a lot of both. It took tremendous effort for me to clean out a five-bedroom, two-bath house in less than two months, sell as much of my belongings as possible, give the rest to the Salvation Army, and stage the house to be sold. Fortunately, I had incredible friends to help me.

On the day I left, it was pouring rain. I remember getting into a taxi with my little Cairn Terrier, Sir London Slattie Bowman, and with him on my lap. I looked out the rearview mirror as we pulled away from my house of 20 years. I was fighting tears and thinking, I don't know what will happen next, but let's go and find out, I was scared to death. I had no place to call home.

The next day, I woke up late at a hotel near the airport and nearly missed my flight to Colorado for the conference. Somehow the flight was miraculously delayed, and I made it. As the plane lifted off, I thought, egad! *I need a hotel room to stay in Colorado!* I had to find living quarters for after the conference. Luckily, I found a great hotel I lived in for several months until I decided on an apartment in Colorado Springs.

In Colorado Springs, I thought about what was next. Okay, you made it to Colorado. Now it's time to initiate the next part of your new life —finding a husband and a new house! But how? I decided to try an online dating app again since so many of my friends had met their mates this way.

Regarding finding a house, I used multiple real estate agents simultaneously in Fort Collins and Colorado Springs. To find a home, I would drive six hours each weekend from the Springs to Fort Collins and look at 10 to 20 houses each trip. To find a husband, I selected an app known for successfully matching spouses —eHarmony.

It took six months to find a house. But within *five days*, the man of my dreams walked into my life through eHarmony. Drop the mic!

I remember every detail of our first date. And Steve Harvey was right. On our third date, I told this man you have a year to propose. I couldn't believe that the words had come out of my mouth. When that year was up, and he hadn't proposed, I thought about what would happen next. Six months later, we were in a jewelry store having a beautiful gold bracelet he had given me repaired. I decided to have my finger sized. I also decided to ask my boyfriend to walk over and take a look at the wedding rings for men. On the way over to that section, he asked, "Do you see any rings you like?" I responded, "well, darlin, these (diamonds) are much too small for me," he smiled.

While he was trying on rings, the salesman said you know, Ms. Bowman, it is very in vogue for women to propose to men these days. That's when I looked at my then-boyfriend and said, "so will you marry me?"

He looked at me and very understatedly said, "sure." WOW! Steve Harvey was right, and that's what I call *courage*. The next chapter in my life started with my being happily married to my silver-haired Italian fox of a man. His wedding vows stopped my heart, as tears of joy rolled down *his* face. I always tell people that I proposed to him, which he gets a kick out, of but in reality, years later I realized he said it first ...I just did not hear him... ***"Are there any rings here that you like?"***

Emotional Courage Behavior

Story #2: "In Search of My Father"

"There is a stubbornness about me that never can bear to be frightened at the will of others. My courage always rises at every attempt to intimidate me."

—Jane Austen, Pride and Prejudice

One day, I was sitting in my teeny studio apartment in Manhattan. Wouldn't *it be nice to see my dad?* My next thought was, *I will go see my dad tomorrow!* I had a date that night and thought I didn't care. I was going to see my dad. I quickly packed my bag, pulled out my credit card, and awaited my date. He had a car. When he arrived, I asked if he could take me to the airport. "He looked at me, confused. "Are we picking somebody up at the airport? Are we double dating?" I said, *"No, I'm going to Panama!"*

He looked shocked and baffled. Then he asked me a million questions: Why are you going? Do you have money to get there? Do you have tickets? How are you getting there? I smiled and calmly replied that I had planned to fly and didn't have tickets. I plan to buy them with my credit card at the airport. I then explained that I was planning to surprise my dad. When my date dropped me off at the airport, he gave me all the cash in his pocket and said you might need more than a credit card. He then laughingly said I was crazy and kissed me good luck.

On the plane, I sat next to a lovely woman. I told her I was going to Panama to find my dad, though I had no idea where to find him. I knew he was on an army base, but that was it. I had no place to stay. I had very little cash. She asked me if I was Panamanian, and I said no. She asked me several more questions: Have you been to Panama? No. Does your dad know you're coming? No. How will you reach him" By phone? She then expressed some concern for me and gave me her phone number. She was kind enough to try and help me find a place to stay. She said, "I know there is a hotel where military families stay. I can take you there so you will be safe." I accepted her help. After settling into the hotel, I excitedly picked up the phone and called the military base, saying I would like to speak to my father, Lieutenant Colonel James C. Bowman. After some back and forth, 20 minutes later, I was on the phone with my dad. And 30 minutes after that, my dad was at my hotel!

The first thing he asked me was, "Does your mother know where you are?" I looked at him, laughed, and said, "probably not, since I didn't tell her I was coming to see you!" He looked at me as though I had three heads and then shook his head while laughing. Next, he said you are crazy, "call your mom NOW, young lady, so she knows where you are." I knew I was going to be in massive trouble with my mom, but it only took a few minutes before we talked to her; she was so confused and upset. I started the conversation by saying, "what's the weather like?" She responded, "we are having a blizzard." I replied, "well, it's sunny and 95 degrees here." She said, "what the hell are you talking about? Where are you?" "In Panama with pop!" My dad poked me, laughing so hard pretending that he was angry. He told my mom I had brought a suitcase filled with winter clothes —meanwhile, it was 95 degrees in Panama! As he winked at me, he told my mom that was part of my devious plan, for him to buy me a new summer wardrobe. I, of course, feigned innocence.

I stayed for two weeks and had the best time of my life learning about a new culture. I saw people living in huts with dirt floors, yet everyone had a TV. I traveled through the rainforest to learn about their ecology...trips into the rainforest were scary and spectacular as the bus driver drove at top speed along the rainforest mountain walls. Then there was the opportunity to learn about their art; I still have the molas I purchased. Of course, I also learned about military life through my dad. It was a great bonding opportunity for both of us. The thoughts and images are still with me today and continue to guide me as I learn about new countries, new cultures, the arts, and the generosity of people.

Would you say that this took courage? I would say yes. Plus, I am a little crazy.

In later years, I revisited Panama on my way to Cuba. To my surprise, so much had changed. The exquisite hotel I had stayed in for American military families was now a hangout for prostitutes. It was clear to me how easily something so magnificent can be destroyed when people no longer care, and I saw first-hand how nothing ever really stays the same.

My dad is now laid to rest in Arlington National Cemetery with my mom—the ultimate burial grounds of the courageous men and women who serve to protect our country.

I share this story with you in hopes you'll have the courage to try something new, despite any adversity you face. *Having courage can lead you to the beginning of new learnings and new experiences, having an appreciation of what was while having an appreciation of what is and what is to come.*

Journal of Microcourage©

Write Your Emotional Behavior Story:

_____

_____

_____

_____

_____

_____

_____

_____

_____

_____

_____

_____

_____

_____

_____

_____

_____

_____

Intellectual Microcourage© Behavior

Story #1: What Happens When You Can't Pass
the Entrance Exam?

"If You Can't Fly, Then Run.
If You Can't Run, Then Walk.
If You Can't Walk, Then Crawl,
But By All Means, Keep Moving."

—Martin Luther King Jr.

I always knew there was something different about me, but I never could figure out quite what it was. I remember my mother going to open school week, which was always around my birthday, and I remember the fear of not getting birthday presents and being punished for not having good grades. My parents were strict about grades, and I did not measure up.

I remember spending many days and nights in my room feeling so sad about my grades and not knowing what to do. I began to hate school with a passion. I remember my mom giving me spelling bees at home while she was sitting at her sewing machine, and each time I got a word wrong, she would pick up the yardstick and hit me over the back of my hand. Do not get me wrong; my mother was one of the best moms. But, in her day, she did not know about dyslexia, and she did not know how to help me achieve excellent grades, and great grades for her were the key to success.

I thought I would die when my parents told me I had to attend college. The last thing I wanted to do was to go to college, more torture! But my parents insisted a college education was necessary; they were willing to take on extra jobs to pay for it. End of discussion! I went to college, but with great trepidation.

I decided to take what seemed like the easy way out and selected a major that I liked. I picked a program where I didn't think I'd have to pass academic exams; I chose to go to Parsons School of Design, where I studied interior design. While there, I won awards for my design work. Following graduation, I remember getting jobs that were so low-level it was embarrassing, but it was all that was offered to me. I remember being in situations where people I reported to claimed my designs as theirs; this wasn't like design school, where I'd won awards and had fun. In school, I was in a cocoon where everyone collaborated and moved towards a common cause of creating the world's next best design.

I quickly realized that my meager income would not allow me to buy the house I so desperately wanted. I finally decided I had to go to graduate school. My apprehension was out of control. I only entertained thoughts of not being able to get into graduate school and of flunking out if I made it into a school. And then there was how I could afford to go.

I knew I'd have to score high on my GMAT to be accepted into a university... and this would likely not happen. Still, I studied hard, took the test, and attended prep classes. However, as predicted, I did poorly.

I sat down one day and decided I would no longer let this setback get in my way. I was going to have the courage to leap and lead myself. I was going to figure out a way to get into graduate school. *But how?*

I thought to myself, *CB, you've worked in the business world and need to use the skills you developed in corporate America to get into graduate school.* So I selected Pace University because they required fewer math requirements in their MBA program, which was my Achilles' heel.

Then, I decided to do something incredibly bold and courageous, knowing I could not rely on my grades alone or do well on the GMATS. I made an appointment to talk with the dean. Granted, I may have misled his administrative assistant by indicating that I was a friend of his to secure an appointment. My strategy worked! However, at the top of the meeting, I confessed my ruse, which the dean found amusing. "If getting into the MBA program is that important to you, we should talk," he said.

I told him how much I wanted to get into graduate school but that my GMAT scores and academic grades could have been better. I even said I'd be willing to go back and take undergraduate classes to improve my grades.

That's when he stopped me and said, "young lady, never go backward; always go forward." Confused, I asked if I could get into graduate school, despite my poor test scores. He responded, "because of your intense desire to get in, I will let you in on probation. You must maintain a C average in your first year. How does that sound?" I was nervous and overjoyed! At the same time. "I'm scared," I confessed, "but I will accept your offer!"

Being tenacious, I decided to take my most challenging classes in my first year to get them out of the way. The first was accounting which took a toll on me intellectually, mentally, and physically. I had so much trouble with my accounting class that I nearly had a nervous breakdown. I remember getting on the bus one night to go home and being so disoriented that I couldn't remember *how* to go home. Fortunately, I had a great bus driver who knew me from taking his bus several nights a week, and he helped me when he saw that I was out of sorts. When I got home, I decided I needed to hire a tutor to get through the class.

My tutor was outstanding. One day, she tested me and said, "I don't understand why you didn't answer these two questions. I know you know the answer because we just discussed them." I looked at her bewildered and asked, "What two questions? She pointed to them, and I responded because I never saw the questions. That's when she asked me if I was dyslexic. I didn't know what that meant; I had never heard of dyslexia. Finally, she explained dyslexia to me and began to look over the past work I had done with her. "I think you have dyslexia and perhaps should get tested."

I took her advice, and the test result turned my life around for the better. I learned that not only was I highly dyslexic, but I also suffered from dyscalculia (duhs·kal·kyoo·lee·uh) which affects your number sense and visual-spatial processing. No wonder I had trouble drawing perspectives in design school! Strangely this was a great relief! I now understood all the difficulties I'd had in school. And having the diagnosis gave me the tools I needed to get through graduate school and life.

Unfortunately, there were times later in my life when I was terminated from jobs for being dyslexic and having dyscalculia. I'd accepted it at first but then became angry. Finally, I decided to push back. I studied how to manage both disabilities AND how to embrace them. I read about dyslexic historians and contemporaries like Octavia Spencer, George Washington, Richard Branson, Whoopi Goldberg, Pablo Picasso, Albert Einstein, Anderson Cooper, Cher, and Charles Schwab, among many others. I realized I was in great company, so it helped me embrace my dyslexia. I am still working on dyscalculia. Sadly, discrimination against people with dyslexia and dyscalculia was not illegal. The Americans with Disability Act came into being in 1990 did not exist at that time.

As the years passed, I realized there were a few things I courageously wanted in dealing with my learning disabilities. This courage included boldly sharing my experience with anyone who would listen. The other was my confidence in letting naysayers own their bias against learning disabilities and understanding that it was their problem – not mine.

My determination became stronger and more critical in opening my firm. Finally, I decided that the first step was to own my dyslexia and my dyscalculia; they would no longer own me.

In embracing my learning disorders, I viewed them as an asset. I began to focus on my advanced skills. Skills that my associates did not possess. Those included communicating with all levels of intellect and various cultures. I can see through people and inspire people to share with me things that they had never or rarely shared with others. I am a great strategist seeing through the rhetoric where others cannot see, I can hear what is not being said, and I am an exceptionally creative problem solver, unlike others. One person excitedly said, "CB, I figured you out." I gently smiled and said, "do tell." I was stunned at the accuracy of his reply, "you see the world as a jigsaw puzzle, and you like putting together the pieces." Later in life, a client gave me a birthday present —a sterling silver jigsaw puzzle! It is sometimes scary at the accuracy; some can see you.

All of these realizations required a great deal of courage. Courage to step out of the quagmire that others had placed me in AND that I had accepted. I've learned that Microcourage© is a platform I own. Like many others, you can enjoy the fruits of Microcourage©! It does not take the form of running into a burning building to save a life; instead, it takes the form of self-appreciation and recognition that we are accomplishing tasks to reach our goal every day, regardless of the simplicity of the purpose.

Intellectual Microcourage©

Story #2: "If You Want a Job? Then Go to The Top"

"You cannot swim for new horizons until you have courage to lose sight of the shore."

—William Faulkner

I remember desperately wanting to find a job but not just *any* job. I wanted a job like my white friends had. I wanted a corporate career with stability, one with all of the glitz, glitter, and glamor.

Yes, I wanted to have all their bells and whistles. My goal was an expense account, travel opportunities, a bigger paycheck, longer vacation time, and an executive coach. However, I soon realized that growing up as a black woman, the child of a military father, and the daughter of a working mother, I didn't know the first thing about *finding* a job. I didn't even know how to write a resume! Or how to write a biographical profile. I never learned about the proper follow-up steps following a job interview. Heck, I didn't even know how to conduct a job interview, and I certainly did not know how to ask for the salary I deserved. I thought people didn't share that kind of information. I was told never to ask people about what they were being paid; it was considered a punishable cardinal sin!

Luckily, I met a black woman named Claire Daniels, who was younger than me but had plenty of corporate experience. She knew the critical steps of finding a job and was a resume-writing expert. I was lucky she took me under her tutelage. I realized with her help that writing a resume was just the *beginning* of the job search.

Claire asked me various questions; where I had worked, my title, the years I'd worked for different companies, did I have staff, et al. Then, the real work began when she asked me to describe my roles —what I did in each position to increase profits and decrease losses for each company where I had worked. Everything I said had to be described quantitatively or qualitatively. Her inquiries felt like getting root canals. I had no idea how to explain what I did in those terms.

She asked me from a measurable perspective so that a potential employer would tell themselves; I *need to hire this person*. However, to me, she was speaking a foreign language. I repeatedly said, "Well, I did this, but I did it with somebody else, or I did that, but I don't know how to translate it into numbers." Finally, she said, "stop, nobody in this world does anything by themselves, so let's eliminate your saying, 'I did this with somebody else.' Just tell me what you did and have the courage to own it!"

I looked at her, stunned. Do *people do that? Isn't it dishonest?* She told me it was commonly understood that people worked with others but stressed how important it was for me to own outcomes as the lead person.

After reeling with that realization, I slowly incorporated phrases like "I was responsible" and "I lead this team" into my language.

The next challenging question Claire asked was, "how would you quantify your results?" Now, this seemed worse than a root canal. This was like a tooth extraction without Novocaine! I looked at her and asked her to define "quantify." I had no idea what she was asking. I knew how to design; how to select furniture and fabrics. I was talented at managing budgets and creating, releasing, and analyzing RFPs. I also knew how to read blueprints and draft floor plans, but I needed to understand how to translate these activities the way she needed.

Claire looked at me gently and smiled. She said, "CB, how much money did you save your clients?" But the problem was that I never realized the importance of tracking these numbers for a job search. "Were you given a budget?" she asked me. Well, of course, I was given a budget. "Did you ever spend more than the budget?" I told her yes! When the client changed the specifications. Then she asked me, "could your clients purchase the same thing you purchased for the same amount?" I was stunned. I said, "hell no! It would have cost them three times the amount!" Clare smiled and said, "CB, now we're talking."

Next, I was taught the other components of a job search, including how to write cover letters and develop a power-packed follow-up campaign. I wanted to help others years later I became a Career Coach. One of the best around! Which led to my moving into the world of outplacement!

Then, the time came for me to display more courage —to move up and into the corporate world, to the big times, into the *Fortune 500 world*. I courageously and confidently updated my resume. I wrote incredible cover letters, designed a brilliant follow-up campaign, and did a mass mailing.

Surprise, surprise —there were no offers. My money was getting thinner and thinner as I approached near-hysteria. I thought, what am I doing wrong? It was clear that I needed additional courage, but what? I had to take a giant leap of faith.

I sat at my typewriter, yes *typewriter*, and wrote to Fortune 500 companies. But this time, I wrote directly to each member of the board of directors and the CEO. In addition, I contacted companies that had previously sent rejections.

In the letter, I said I was a perfect fit for their company, described my strengths, and requested an interview. This strategy resulted in my receiving letters from a few companies requesting an interview, which resulted in job offers!

Many years later, after working at one of the organizations, I ran into the person who had sent me a rejection letter. I loved mentioning that he had not invited me in for an interview. He looked at me and said, "Clearly that was *my* mistake." Twenty years later, I was still working at the company. Fast forward after I left, I opened my firm; ironically, this person connected with me to come to work with me on an initiative.

Courage? *Oh yes, I was courageous.*

Journal of Microcourage©

Write Your Intellectual Behavior Story:

_____

_____

_____

_____

_____

_____

_____

_____

_____

_____

_____

_____

_____

_____

_____

_____

_____

_____

Spiritual Microcourage©

Story: A Black Woman in a Synagogue in Turkey

"Courage is contagious. When a brave man takes a stand, the spines of others are stiffened."

—Rev. Billy Graham

What is it like to be the only black person to walk into a synagogue? What is it like to be the only black person celebrating a Bar Mitzvah? What is it like to be the only black person walking through the Istanbul markets and receiving a marriage proposal?

Ask me because I have been that person. I have had people smile at me, I have had people look at me with curiosity, and I have had children hide because of my skin color. But, has that stopped me from being inquisitive right back at them, a kind of inquisitiveness that allowed me to widen my knowledge of other people, places, hearts, and religions? No.

To me, walking the streets of Istanbul or attending a bar mitzvah did not take courage, yet to others, it could be perceived as being courageous or just plain crazy. However, I categorize this as a *thirst for knowledge*. A knowledge that allows me to participate at a deeper level with friends, family, colleagues, and even strangers. For example, after I visited Japan and China, I observed what I believed to be rude behavior—extreme aggressiveness when it came to personal space in public areas. However, when I observed that there were people hired to push people onto a train; so that everybody could get on board, I realized that it was not rudeness. The realization came that people of these countries see space as a precious commodity. My translation of this activity was that the behavior resulted from their the tiny landmass vis-à-vis population size, I understood that it was a cultural thing based on fundamental necessity.

Looking back, I realize the courage was in my taking the journey itself. Courage allowed me to experience being in a foreign country, without speaking the language, and being of a different race. And let's not forget being a young woman alone. I had no idea how I would be perceived or treated, and there would be no one to turn to should I need help. However, *"the courage to learn superseded the fear of ignorance."*

I remember going to my first bar mitzvah, and as I sat there and tried to sing the songs the others were singing, I began to feel the same pride that my friends felt as they watched their little boy become a man. I certainly didn't understand the words I was trying to sing, but I understood this religion's feeling and richness.

What an extraordinary experience! I remember leaving the service to attend the celebratory dinner, where many people came up smiling and welcoming me to their synagogue. One of the guests asked me if I knew the words and the meaning of the songs and the spoken words. My response was no, but I knew the importance of the ceremony to my friend Miriam Clark and her family, and I knew the heart of the words.

Spiritual courage is brutal to describe and not necessarily related to religion, as I've presented it here. In 2014 Sandra Ford Walston wrote in an article entitled "Courage Is Caged in the Workplace" for CLO, she stated, "The spiritual journey requires being present to presence. It is a trust in faith that propels you to continue growing. You become a witness to your 'attachments to results' and learn to self-correct. You surrender your ego to a higher level of consciousness where courage meets grace. As this happens, humility steps in to replace arrogance and righteousness."

Indeed, I've read many definitions, and they all are centered around recognizing a higher authority. For me, it was presented by going to a different religious event, sharing the experience of being proud of my friend's son, and understanding the joy brought to his parents.

I also remember my first Italian Thanksgiving and Christmas. Oh boy! Was it ever fun to learn about and enjoy the "Feast of the Seven Fishes." For many Italian-Americans, the Feast—a nostalgia-fueled, hours-long dinner consisting of at least seven different types of fish and seafood—is the defining Christmas Eve tradition that *brings luck in the New Year and* remembrance, faith, and love of family, good times and good food. Of course, fish being my favorite food; I was all in!

I list many experiences related to having the courage to learn about different cultures. In addition to learning about the behavior related to other cultures, the fun has been learning about food. Yes, I am guilty of merging courage and behavior with culture with the pleasure of eating.

Here I presented stories related to what we commonly think of as spiritual. However, examining the levels will also show my values, beliefs, and morals. Having experiences that allowed me to "see people" afforded me more compassion for understanding different behaviors of teams and colleagues, especially how they show up in times of crisis. For example, during Covid, I immediately realized I was fortunate to be introverted. I could stay alone comfortably for much longer than most people, but given that introversion represented less than 25% of the members of my association —the Association of Corporate Executive Coaches —I needed a call to action to support the extroverts.

As a result of Covid, the members were starving for non-Covid related news, missing a sense of belonging, and missing client activity due to the isolation mandates requiring them to stay home. From my experience understanding what was important to different people and my experience as a leader, I knew I had to offer members a collaborative opportunity. Therefore, I created Zoom Saturday morning fireside chats, which were exceptionally well attended and deeply appreciated. However, attendance dropped when we returned to the "new normal" following covid, so we dispensed the fireside chat; *its importance had diminished.*

You might think that spirituality would not fall into the arena of courage, but spiritual behavior in the business world refers to the art of leadership. **The spiritual leader emerges when we dare to align with our values, beliefs, and morals – even if doing so may be difficult or unpopular.**

Journal of Microcourage©

Write Your Spiritual Behavior Story:

_____

_____

_____

_____

_____

_____

_____

_____

_____

_____

_____

_____

_____

_____

_____

_____

_____

_____

Another View

In Sally Helgesen's book *Rising Together How We Can Bridge Divides and Create a More Inclusive Workplace*, she looks at behavior in creating synergy across gender, age, ethnicity, race, sexuality, and life experience. Sally identifies negative triggers which play havoc with the way we think and how this depletes our courage muscle. These triggers are widespread yet rarely acknowledged. They include differences in how people from different backgrounds view ambition, competence, perceptions, fairness, communication, etc.

The courage to explore, examine, acknowledge, and accept others strengthens our courage muscle. Enhancing our knowledge of others creates a broader avenue for collaboration and cooperation. **It allows us to expand our network and creates a more substantial barrier against failure.**

SECTION 2

~

Implementing Courage

The Yellow Brick Road

This section will provide a roadmap for using the Microcourage©
process to broaden your leadership skills. Presented is a
seven-step process for turning perceived and current failures
into realized success. As you take the journey, I remind you that
leadership is not a title. It is a mindset that is required at every
level of the organization.

*"And the day came when the risk to remain tight in a
bud was more painful than the risk it took to blossom."*

—Anais Nin

MICROCOURAGE© ROAD MAP

STEP 1: TO EXERT: *Courage to step out of the quagmire*

Definition of Exert

*ex·ert | \ ig-'zərt *

- *to put forth (strength, effort, etc.)*
- *to put (oneself) into action*
- *to bring to bear, especially with sustained effort or lasting effect.*

EXERT: Relationship to Microcourage©:

Being stuck in a quagmire —one that you didn't even know existed —prevents us from exerting the courage to make bold decisions, lead confidently, and solve our most intractable problems. *It prevents us from doing brave work, such as seeing and admitting that we are stuck in a quagmire.* We stop trying because our skills have not kept up with the pace of change. We don't believe we can grow and learn anymore. We aren't even sure what the right thing to do is anymore, *so why bother?* In the implementation of courage, it is critical to examine the restraints that are the cause of being in a quagmire. The workplace today is filled with questions, complications, and predicaments —even if you're not in one right now, you probably know someone who is.

It is natural not to face our fears if we can't think of any way out. As a result, the situation seems hopeless. We may have tried avoidance, but we find that even that has yet to work. Quagmires are when people feel stuck in any part of their life. They hang on day after day, clinging to routines and habits rather than facing up to new ways of doing things. Everyone in a quagmire begins to feel like victims, with no choice but to keep going in the same direction—even if it leads them over a cliff.

The ironic part is that when you're stuck in a quagmire, it's easy to forget what you are capable of dissipating the predicament. Temporary blindness happens to just about everyone. You can become overwhelmed by the circumstances and paralyzed by the enormity of your situation. The good news is that there are plenty of ways to fight back—you have to know how. *Knowing we are in a quagmire is the first step in getting out!* [1]

Strategic thinking comes in very handy. It allows you to step out of the quagmire when you take an honest, deep look at *"What Got You Here,"* to quote Marshall Goldsmith, determine where you want to go, *and* determine your "why," to quote Simon Sinek. These steps will allow you to look at the interrelationship between what you will need to get you to your goal and your expected results. Include in your strategic thinking whom you will need support from, what kind of support you will need, and when you will need the help. Most importantly, you need to answer the following two questions.

> *"What will failure look like and what important steps would be needed to turn failure into success."*

> **—CB Bowman**

Remember that success redefined can be as simple as what you learn. While this type of strategic thinking may seem daunting at first glance I promise it will become robotic when used consistently.

These are all potent and frightful questions that can cause any of us to stop in our track's versus having the Microcourage.©

---

[1] *A warning when you pull out of a quagmire, you are susceptible to "quagmire flashback"! This flashback happens when something small or non-related pulls you back into the trap, even for a very short time. We must be careful at these times because these flashbacks are energy drainers. There are only so many times you can recharge a battery.*

to move forward. However, once answered you will be provided with a security blanket that will support your journey of *Courage to Leap & Lead.*

Here are some ways you can use **Step 1** to mitigate the quagmire and build your courage:

1. **Break the situation down:** Quagmire situations can be overwhelming, but breaking them down into smaller, more manageable pieces can help you build the courage to tackle them. Identify the specific challenges and obstacles you are facing, and develop a plan for how to address each one.

2. **Be open to new perspectives:** Quagmire situations often require creative solutions and new perspectives. Be open to new ideas and approaches, and don't be afraid to think outside the box. By being open to new perspectives, you can build the courage to take risks and try new things.

3. **Build your knowledge and skills:** Quagmire situations often require specialized knowledge and skills. Take time to develop your expertise and build your confidence in your abilities. By building your knowledge and skills, you can build the resilience and courage to tackle even the most difficult challenges.

4. **Seek support:** Quagmire situations can be isolating, but seeking out support from others can help you build the courage to overcome them. Reach out to friends, family, or a professional support system for help and guidance. By seeking support, you can build the resilience and courage you need to overcome obstacles and pursue success.

5. **Practice self-care:** Quagmire situations can be stressful and overwhelming, but practicing self-care can help you build the resilience and courage you need to persevere. Take care of your physical and emotional health,

and develop coping strategies to help you deal with stress and adversity.

6. **Celebrate progress:** Quagmire situations often require persistence and perseverance, and it's important to celebrate your progress along the way. Acknowledge your accomplishments and give yourself credit for your hard work and progress. By celebrating your successes, you can build the confidence and motivation you need to keep moving forward.

"The answer is the beginning of the question."

—CB Bowman

STEP 2: TO EXPLORE: *Courage to deep test/ apply critical thinking concepts with a no blame, no shame, no guilt approach*

Definition of Explore

*ex·plore | \ ik-'splȯr *

- to investigate, study, or analyze
- to become familiar with by testing or experimenting
- to travel over (new territory) for adventure or discovery
- to examine, especially for diagnostic purposes

(Focus on exterior triggers and influences.)

EXPLORE: Relationship To Microcourage©:

Courage requires exploration because it often involves facing fears or challenging circumstances. As we explore, we encounter new experiences and challenges that may require us to be brave and take risks. For example, a job interview, trying a new hobby, or speaking up in a challenging conversation may all require us to step outside our comfort zone and have the courage to face the unknown.

Courage also requires exploration because it involves facing our fears or challenging circumstances that we may not have encountered before. We need to use "exploration" to understand quagmires. We must be open to new experiences and willing to take risks to achieve our goals.

Exploring and courage reinforce one another. When we explore, we often encounter challenges that require us to be brave and have the courage to overcome them. Similarly, when we dare to face our fears and challenges, we often open ourselves up to new experiences and opportunities for exploration. We open ourselves up to new solutions that we had not imagined before.

Here are some specific steps for using **Step 2 "Explore"** to build your courage and turn failure into success:

1. **Embrace the unknown:** One of the biggest obstacles to exploring new territory is the fear of the unknown. It can be daunting to step into unfamiliar territory, but it is often where the most significant opportunities for growth and success lie. By embracing the unknown, you can build courage to take risks and pursue new opportunities.

2. **Learn from failure:** Failure is a natural part of exploring new territory. It can be discouraging to experience setbacks, but it is essential to learn from them and use them as opportunities for growth. By reframing failure as a learning experience, you can build the resilience and courage you need to persevere in the face of obstacles.

3. **Take small steps:** Exploring new territory can be overwhelming, but taking small steps can help build your confidence and courage. Start by setting small goals and celebrating each success along the way. As you gain momentum, you will feel more empowered to take on bigger challenges.

4. **Seek new experiences:** The more you expose yourself to new experiences, the more comfortable you will become with the unknown. Seek out opportunities to try new things, whether learning a new skill, exploring a new place, or meeting new people. By broadening your horizons, you will build your courage and expand your perspective.

5. **Surround yourself with support:** Exploring new territory can be lonely and isolating, but having a support system can make all the difference. Surround yourself with people who encourage and support you, and who are willing to help you navigate the challenges of exploration. Having a solid support system will make you feel more confident and courageous in your pursuit of success.

6. **Celebrate success:** Celebrating your accomplishments along the way is essential, no matter how small they may seem. Acknowledge your progress and credit yourself for the hard work and courage it takes to explore new territory. By celebrating your successes, you will build the confidence and motivation you need to keep moving forward.

STEP 3: TO EXAMINE: *Courage to inspect and identify roadblocks and triggers*

Definition of Examine
ex·am·ine | \ ig'zamən \

- inspect (someone or something) in detail to determine their nature or condition; investigate thoroughly
- to select a roadblock and identify your most critical quagmires

(Focus on exterior triggers and influences.)

EXAMINE: Relationship to Microcourage©:

Asking questions, seeking new ideas, and exploring possibilities open your mind to new ways of approaching and executing things. The more you know, the more options you have for making decisions. You'll become more confident and effective in making those decisions. Asking questions, seeking new ideas, and exploring possibilities increase your ability to have the best possible outcomes before moving forward with new initiatives or moving away from those that have failed. This process is critical to step out of the quagmire. **Remember, analysis is not paralysis when the research is propelling you forward.** It is that branch on the mighty oak tree you can grab onto to pull yourself out of sinking further into the quicksand.

As a leader, you must define and create the kind of work environment and culture that allows employees to be courageous which includes equal space for failure and success. This can mean addressing implicit bias in hiring practices, creating processes around career development, implementing mentorship programs within your team, and or creating new services/ products.

Here are some specific steps for using **Step 3 "to examine"** in building courage and turning failure into success:

1. **Identify your fears:** Examining your fears can help you understand what is holding you back and how to address those fears. Take some time to reflect on what you are afraid of and why. Once you have identified your fears, you can develop a plan to overcome them.

2. **Analyze your mistakes:** Examining your mistakes can help you learn from them and avoid making the same mistakes in the future. Take a critical look at your past

failures and analyze what went wrong. Use this information to develop a plan for how to improve and avoid similar mistakes in the future.

3. **Evaluate your strengths:** Examining your strengths can help you build the confidence and courage you need to pursue success. Take time to reflect on what you are good at and what makes you unique. By focusing on your strengths, you can build your confidence and find the courage to take on new challenges.

4. **Consider your options:** Examining your options can help you identify new opportunities and approaches for success. Take a step back and consider all your options, even ones that may seem unconventional or risky. By examining all of your options, you may find new ways to turn failure into success.

5. **Manage your expectations:** Examining your expectations can help you set realistic goals and avoid becoming discouraged by setbacks. Take a realistic look at what you can achieve and set goals that are challenging but achievable. By managing your expectations, you can avoid becoming discouraged by setbacks and stay focused on your path to success.

6. **Seek feedback:** Examining feedback from others can help you identify areas for improvement and build your confidence. Seek feedback from trusted friends, colleagues, or mentors. Use this feedback to identify areas where you can improve and develop a plan to address those areas.

"There isn't a train I wouldn't take, no matter where it's going."
—Edna Millay

STEP 4: TO EXPRESS: *Courage© to speak out*

Definition of express
\ ik-'spres \

- to represent in words
- to make known the opinions or feelings of (oneself)
- to give or convey a true impression of
- delineate, depict
- to speak loud enough to be heard: to speak boldly and express an opinion frankly
- spoke out on the issues

EXPRESS: The Relationship to Microcourage©:

Why do some speak around a subject, hiding or never getting to the point, whereas others speak out about an issue clearly and purposefully? I'm sure thousands of studies explain this behavior, but it doesn't matter why. The courage to speak out and to ask for help is the easiest way to develop your courage muscle. Realizing that you are not alone and giving homage to the expression "two heads are better than one" is a significant factor in gaining courage.

When we stand up and speak out, we are on the road to courageousness, and we are eliciting support from others. We are inviting others to listen. Notice I did not say we are getting people to agree because we don't want everyone to agree. We want people to listen and speak their true north. We are sharing our stories. We aim for respect and support, and as long as we are not annoyingly kvetching, we should be able to reach that critical goal. Others will listen if you intend to solve, share, create, or innovate. When you dare to share and listen, you can prevent yourself from making decisions that could be harmful to you or others. Don't stick your head in the sand and ignore

In life, small teams, and organizations of every size, speaking up or " jumping in" is an essential learned skill in being courageous. Give yourself the gift of confidence to speak up without fear of reprisal, to express your thoughts and concerns, to support yourself, or to support others. Speaking up can take on many different forms of communication. It is best to discover the type of communication that works well with your style and the person you want to engage. For example, how do they like to receive information —by telephone, email, text, visual, audio, or other? In what form do they like to receive information — detailed, summarized, outlined, et al.? How do you want them to respond, and can they respond in a way that you need them to so you understand their response completely?

You need to be able to speak out and stand up for what you believe in, whether standing up to a manager trying to put you in an impossible situation or voicing your opinion about a product or policy that could do good or harm, even questioning your abilities can play a vital role. The ability to debate, hear all sides, and conclude is courage.

Here are some specific steps for using **Step 4 "to express"** in building your courage and turning failure into success:

1. **Acknowledge your feelings:** Expressing your feelings can help you process and overcome the fear of failure. Take some time to acknowledge and express your emotions, whether it's through journaling, talking with a friend, or seeking professional help. By acknowledging your feelings, you can work through them and build the resilience you need to overcome setbacks.

2. **Share your story:** Sharing your story with others can help you build your courage and inspire others facing similar challenges. Whether through social media, blogging, or speaking publicly, sharing your experiences can help you find purpose and meaning in your struggles.

3. **Practice self-compassion:** Expressing self-compassion can help you build the courage to persevere in the face of failure. Be kind and gentle with yourself, and avoid self-criticism and negative self-talk. By practicing self-compassion, you can build the resilience and courage to overcome setbacks and pursue success.

4. **Set boundaries:** Expressing your needs and setting boundaries can help you build the courage to prioritize your well-being and avoid burnout. Step back and identify what you need to feel supported and successful. Then, communicate these needs clearly and set boundaries to protect your time and energy.

5. **Celebrate progress:** Expressing gratitude and celebrating progress can help you build the confidence and courage you need to pursue success. Take time to reflect on your accomplishments, no matter how small they may seem. You can create the motivation and momentum to keep moving forward by expressing gratitude and celebrating progress.

6. **Seek support:** Expressing your need for support can help you build the courage to ask for help and avoid feeling isolated. Contact friends, family, or a professional support system for help and guidance. You can create the resilience and courage to overcome setbacks and pursue success by expressing your need for support.

In summary, expressing your feelings, sharing your story, practicing self-compassion, setting boundaries, celebrating progress, and seeking support can help you build the courage to turn failure into success.

"Speak every time you stand so you don't forget yourself."

—Anis Mojgani "Shake the Dust"

STEP 5: TO ENGAGE: *Courage to* <u>*listen, accept*</u> *help, and* <u>*acknowledge*</u> *the help received.*

Definition of Engage
en·gage | \ in-'gāj, en- \ engaged; engaging

- to get involved with other people and their ideas in order to understand their ideas
- to interest someone in something and keep them thinking about it

ENGAGE: Relationship to Microcourage©:

Every day, we see people making a difference and doing their best. However, people must realize their power to create *more* impact. Having the courage to leap and lead allows teams and individuals to explore how they can do more by breaking through barriers and taking risks. In addition, having the confidence that comes from knowing you are valued as a thinking and courageous human is powerful. It includes accepting help and the *courage to acknowledge the support you receive from those with whom you engage.*

This critical ability makes generating momentum, overcoming obstacles, and gaining traction nearly possible. Individuals can work together in a collaborative environment and face challenges and new opportunities head-on when engaged.

The essential condition for being courageous is initiating and leading the way, standing up for yourself, celebrating your beliefs and opinions, and having *internal security.* Courage emerges from a sense of self-worth. If you believe you are worthy of living a whole life and achieving your goals, you have the confidence to take risks, take action, and be an agent of change. Then courage will be as easy as slicing softened butter.

Courage to seek help and the courage to accept help includes several factors, including:

- Facing your reality
- Discovering who you are
- Identifying your triggers
- Knowing your why
- Identifying your resources
- Knowing your how
- Knowing your pitch to make it happen
- Knowing your target market
- Knowing your allies and adversaries
- Knowing your roadblocks
- Not being afraid to explore lack of success

Here are some specific steps for **Step 5:** using **"engage"** to build your courage and turn failure into success:

1. **Take responsibility:** Engaging with your situation requires taking responsibility for your actions and outcomes. Acknowledge your role in the situation and take ownership of your mistakes. By taking responsibility, you can build the courage to learn from your failures and take action to improve.

2. **Set goals:** Engaging with your situation requires setting clear and achievable goals. Identify what you want to achieve and develop a plan for how to get there. By setting goals, you can build the courage to take action and move forward, even in the face of setbacks.

3. **Take action:** Engaging with your situation requires effort, even when difficult or uncomfortable. Take small

steps toward your goals, even if they seem insignificant. Taking action can build the momentum and confidence you need to overcome obstacles and pursue success.

4. **Seek feedback:** Engaging with your situation requires seeking input from others to identify areas for improvement. For example, ask for feedback from trusted friends, colleagues, or mentors. Use this feedback to identify areas where you can improve and develop a plan to address those areas.

5. **Learn from failures:** Engaging with your situation requires learning from your failures and mistakes. Take a critical look at what went wrong and use this information to improve your approach. By learning from your failures, you can build the resilience and courage you need to persevere in facing obstacles.

6. **Persevere:** Engaging with your situation requires perseverance and resilience. Keep moving forward, even when it's difficult or uncomfortable. You can build the courage to overcome setbacks and pursue success by persevering.

> *"Ask and it will be given to you*
> *Seek and you will find;*
> *Knock and the door will open for you."*
> **—Mathew 7:7**

STEP 6: TO EXECUTE: *The courage to be right or wrong*

Definition of Execute
*ex·e·cute | \ 'ek-si-ˌkyüt *

- to carry out fully: put entirely into effect
- to do what is provided or required
- to make or produce

EXECUTE: Relationship to Microcourage©:

Executing with courage is a vital leadership skill. It enables the leader to take control of situations and to adapt when changes occur, but it's often easier said than done.

The courage to leap and lead is the ability to execute the right decision for the most involved. It's about knowing what needs to be done and *doing it*. It is putting your plan into action, one step at a time, and overcoming fear and self-doubt.

> *"Courageous decision making is*
> *learning how to use your personal strengths,*
> *as well as the strengths of others around you,*
> *this is the gold standard for courageous leadership."*
>
> **—CB Bowman**

Ideas and inspiration come and go; it takes knowing the right decision versus the wrong decision for the greater good and then taking the correct actions to make things happen. Be willing to step forward and create something new —even if you are initially uncomfortable. It is the ability to carry out a task, persist in a difficult situation, or make a decision that is not popular. Execute is performing a plan of action with care and skill. Courageous leaders are those who emotionally and logically understand risks yet are willing to take *calculated risks* and remain deliberate. A leader needs not just the courage to step forward but also the courage to follow through with actions that must be taken.

Execution is not just about carrying out or implementing a plan, order, or course of action. It is also when you dare to stand alone in the face of failure. This action is what makes a true leader.

Here are some specific steps for **<u>Step 6</u>** using **"execution"** to build your courage:

1. **Take action:** Executing your plans requires effort, even when difficult or uncomfortable. Don't let fear hold you back from pursuing your goals. Instead, take small steps toward your goals, even if they seem insignificant. Taking action can build the momentum and confidence you need to overcome obstacles and pursue success.

2. **Embrace the possibility of failure:** Executing your plans requires embracing failure. Recognize that failure is a natural part of achieving success, and use failure as an opportunity to learn and improve. By embracing the possibility of failure, you can build the resilience and courage you need to persevere in the face of obstacles.

3. **Trust your instincts:** Executing your plans requires trusting your instincts and taking risks. Listen to your inner voice and follow your intuition. Sometimes the right decision differs from the popular one, but trusting your instincts can build the confidence and courage you need to take risks and pursue your goals.

4. **Be adaptable:** Executing your plans requires being versatile and flexible. Recognize that plans may need to change as circumstances change, and be willing to pivot and adjust your approach. Being adaptable can build the resilience and courage you need to overcome setbacks and pursue success.

5. **Learn from mistakes:** Executing your plans requires learning from your mistakes and failures. Take a critical look at what went wrong and use this information to improve your approach. By learning from your mistakes, you can build the resilience and courage you need to persevere in facing obstacles.

6. **Celebrate accomplishments:** Executing your plans requires celebrating your successes, no matter how small

they may seem. Recognize and acknowledge your accomplishments and credit yourself for your hard work and progress. Celebrating your successes can build the confidence and motivation you need to keep moving forward.

"How can right be right and wrong be wrong
when sometimes right is wrong and wrong is right?
In my view there is no need for conflict.
Choose your rights and choose your wrongs.
Find that place of balance between the two opposing
views. Live your life from that place.
That place I call, Self."

—M.N. Hopkins

STEP 7: TO RESURGE: *Courage to stand up, stand-alone, and try again*

Definition of Resurge
re·surge | \ ri-ˈsərj \

- to undergo a resurgence
  re·sur·gence | \ ri-ˈsər-jən(t)s \

- a rising again into life, activity, or prominence

Relationship to Microcourage©2

Resurging to rise again from an unexpected and devastating event requires the standard four dimensions of empowerment: meaning, competence, self-determination, and impact. To rise again after devastation, you must possess these qualities plus courage.

---

[2] *To rise like a phoenix from the ashes means to emerge stronger, smarter, and more powerful from a catastrophe. Someone who opens a new, successful business after the previous company has failed.*

Both resurge and courage are closely aligned. When a person embarks on the recovery journey, they will encounter challenges and disappointments. At various times, they may feel like giving up. However, strength in having courage will allow you to push through enormous odds.

Here are some ways you can use **Step 7** to **"resurge"** to build your courage and turn failure into success:

1. **Stand up:** Resurging after a failure requires standing up and taking ownership of your situation. Don't let failure define you or hold you back from pursuing your goals. Instead, stand up and take action to move forward, even in the face of setbacks.

2. **Stand-alone:** Resurging after a failure requires the courage to stand alone and pursue your goals, even if others doubt you. Be confident in your abilities and trust your instincts. Don't let the opinions of others hold you back from pursuing your dreams.

3. **Try again:** Resurging after a failure requires courage, even if you have failed before. Use your past failures as an opportunity to learn and improve. Develop a new action plan and try again with renewed determination and courage.

4. **Stay positive:** Resurging after a failure requires staying positive and focusing on the future. Refrain from dwelling on past failures or negative experiences. Instead, keep a positive attitude and focus on the possibilities and opportunities ahead.

5. **Build resilience:** Resurging after a failure requires building strength and developing the courage to persevere in facing obstacles. Take care of your physical and emotional health, and develop coping strategies to help you deal with stress and adversity.

6. Seek support: Resurging after a failure requires seeking approval from others who can encourage and guide you. Seek friends, family, or a professional support system for help and guidance. You can build the resilience and courage to overcome setbacks and pursue success by seeking support.

To resurge after a failure requires standing up, standing alone, and trying again with renewed determination. The courage to leap & lead can be terrifying. But it opens the door to success for anyone courageous enough to enter.[3] ***Love your fear, embrace and listen to it, but don't let it rule you.***

"Lying, thinking last night
How to find my soul a home
Where water is not thirsty
And bread loaf is not stone
I came up with one thing
And I don't believe I'm wrong
That nobody, But nobody
Can make it out here alone."

—Alone Stanza #1

Maya Angelou - 1928-2014 From *Oh Pray My Wings Are Gonna Fit Me Well* by Maya Angelou. Copyright © 1975 by Maya Angelou.

---

[3] *Once successful we must be careful not to fall into the "paradox of success". The paradox of success was first coined by American psychologist and author, John R. Kimberly, in his 1976 book "The Politics of the Management of Change". In the book, Kimberly discusses how success can create its own set of problems and challenges, and how organizations can become complacent and resistant to change as a result. Since then, the concept of the paradox of success has been widely used and discussed in various fields, including business, psychology, and sociology.*

The Toolbox

TOOLS TO IMPLEMENT COURAGE:

In reality, there are many tools and methods to increase your Microcourage© muscle both in the workplace and in your personal life. They can help guard against failure in the way that failure is defined traditionally, filled with doom and gloom—for example, a mindset shift. Dr. Ana Melikian's book *MINDSET ZONE: Actualize Your Fullest Potential*, Dr. Melikian, explores what mindsets are, how they work, and how we can use them to expand the realm of possibility in our life and work.

A mindset is an essential determinant of courage. When we have a fixed mindset about failure, we believe we are destined for defeat. In contrast, having a growth mindset enables us to think about our abilities and goals more objectively and realistically— which can help shape our courage. There is no courage without a mindset shift from destructive to constructive; a positive mindset can help you face challenges and thrive. According to author Joseph Campbell, courage is "the power of the human spirit to reach beyond the unknown and grapple with the 'world' that is there for each person."

If you are on a team, for example, one standard tool in corporate America is to front-load votes for your new idea by positively influencing the mindset of team members in favor of your vision *before* a group vote.

Other problem-solving business tools include:

- Strategic Thinking
- The Five Whys process
- SWOT Analysis
- Fishbone Chart

Strategic Thinking

Strategic thinking is critical to any organization's success because it focuses on long-term planning and decision-making, enabling leaders to shape their future actions. It also requires courage, as it can involve taking action on ideas that may be unpopular or simply unpopular within the group. The skills related to critical thinking are among the most highly sought-after management competencies. Why? Because employees capable of thinking critically, logically, and strategically can have a tremendous impact on a business's trajectory

Recognizing your Microcourage© helps you identify your skills to think critically. If you want to improve your skills, the good news is that using the skills and the tools listed below will help you increase your proficiency quickly.

Here are three ways to improve your skills:

1. **Be inquisitive.** Asking many questions helps prepare you for surprises and allows you to move forward faster and recover from setbacks more quickly.

2. **Be aware and process information.** Those "what if" scenarios can be a lifeline (as long as you consider only the facts) versus putting your head in the sand.

3. **Both informal and formal training** can prevent common unforeseen errors, i.e., the proper allocation of money, hiring the right employees, how to lead using your true north, and learning applicable laws which will affect your goals.

The Five Whys

The Five Whys is a problem-solving technique that has been around for decades and is often associated with the Toyota Production System. It is a simple but powerful method for getting to the root cause of a problem by asking "why" five times. By repeatedly asking this question, you can uncover underlying issues and identify solutions that may have yet to be apparent.

The Five Whys can help us confront our fears and take action. Avoiding or putting it off can be tempting when faced with a problem or challenge. For example, we may fear failure, the unknown, or how to proceed. Using The Five Whys, we can dig deeper and uncover the underlying reasons for our reluctance to act. For example, let's say we are considering starting a new business but are hesitant to take the first step. By asking ourselves "why" five times, we might uncover that our fear is rooted in a lack of experience, a fear of financial insecurity, or failure. Once we have identified these underlying concerns, we can address them and take steps toward our goal.

Essential for courage is asking "why," which helps us develop a growth mindset. A growth mindset believes we can develop our abilities through hard work and dedication. By asking "why" and uncovering a problem's root cause, we acknowledge that there is room for improvement and that we have the power to make changes. This mindset encourages us to take risks and try new things, even if we are unsure of the outcome.

Secondly, The Five Whys can help us overcome resistance and overcome obstacles. When we encounter resistance or obstacles in our personal or professional lives, it can be easy to give up or become discouraged. However, using The Five Whys, we can uncover the underlying reasons for this resistance and develop strategies to overcome it. For example, let's say we are trying to implement a new process at work, but we need support from our colleagues, which has yet to be forthcoming. By asking "why" five times, we might uncover that the resistance is rooted in fear of change, a lack of understanding of the new process, or a fear of failure. Once we have identified these underlying concerns, we can develop strategies to address them, such as providing training or communication about the benefits of the new process. We can push through resistance and achieve our goals by overcoming these obstacles.

The Five Whys can help us make more courageous decisions by forcing us to consider the consequences of our actions. When making important decisions, it can be easy to focus on short-term outcomes and overlook the long-term effects. By asking "why" five times, we can uncover the underlying reasons for our decision and consider its potential impact. For example, let's say we are considering quitting our job to start a new business. By asking "why" five times, we might uncover that our underlying reason is a desire for more flexibility and control over our work. However, we might also discover concerns about financial stability or the potential impact on our relationships.

Considering these underlying factors, we can make a more informed decision considering both short-term and long-term consequences. For example, if you received a speeding ticket on your way to work and were pulled over by the police, they might ask you why you were speeding. Your answer might be, "because I'm late to work." Using the five whys would determine that you were late for work because you forgot to put batteries in your alarm clock! Here is a detailed example:

1. QUESTION 1: Why were you speeding?
   Response 1: I was late for work.

2. QUESTION 2: Why were you late for work?
   Response 2: My alarm clock didn't go off.

3. QUESTION 3: Why didn't your alarm clock go off?
   Response 3: The batteries needed to be updated.

4. QUESTION 4: Why were the batteries outdated?

Response 4: I just remembered that I had to put in new batteries.

5. QUESTION 5: Why did you forget to install new batteries?

Response 5: I didn't put them on my shopping list.

When we analyze the reasoning behind your getting a speeding ticket, we realize you were late to work because you did not create a shopping list that included *buying batteries*. We could come up with a few more reasons to get to the root cause of *why* you forgot to put batteries on the shopping list, but you get the idea of how useful this tool can be. Here is another scenario you can use this process: to determine what is *preventing* you from utilizing a particular employee on a specific project. Knowing this information will help you increase your courage to identify the best fit for the assignment. In this case, the methodology allows you to identify and eliminate the blockage preventing you from identifying the best candidate. You are exploring the cause and effect of a belief or situation to eliminate barriers to a successful hire or outcome.

Here is another example:

You are concerned about releasing a new product or service.

- Why? Are you concerned about a new product release?

- Why? It could be a significant financial loss to your organization as well as a loss of prestige, loss of market share, and loss of customer loyalty.

- Why? Your competition has a foothold in this service or product.

- Why? Because they came out with it first because they had less to lose.

- Why? Because they were the pioneers in the market.

You might want to add additional steps because we realized we needed more information —now that we know the risk ahead of time, we can plan for them. For example, if you wanted to produce a more innovative product or approach, with less expense, than your competitor by using a *"Blue Ocean Strategy."*

SWOT Analysis

SWOT stands for:

1. **S = Strengths:** This relates to *the internal advantages* you have over others. By identifying strengths, you can gain confidence in your abilities and feel more courageous. Knowing what you are good at can help you to take risks and pursue opportunities that align with your strengths. You can use your strengths to your advantage and overcome challenges and obstacles.

2. **W = Weakness:** This relates to *internal disadvantages* in relation to others. Acknowledging your weaknesses requires courage because it involves admitting to areas where improvement is needed. However, by identifying these weaknesses, you can work on them and become better. You can seek opportunities to learn, grow and become more resilient in the face of challenges.

3. **O = Opportunities:** This relates to the *advantages* you have over others. To benefit from "Opportunities," requires being open-minded and receptive to new ideas and possibilities. It requires courage to take advantage of opportunities, especially stepping out of one's comfort zone. By recognizing opportunities and taking action, you can learn new skills and gain valuable experiences to enhance your personal and professional growth.

4. **T = Threats:** This relates to _external factors_ that could jeopardize the success of your goals. Assessing the threats requires being proactive and prepared for potential challenges and risks. It requires courage to face possible threats and take steps to mitigate them.

Using a SWOT analysis can support you in being courageous by providing a structured way of thinking about your situation, problem, or decision. Sometimes, when faced with a difficult decision or situation, knowing where to start can be overwhelming and challenging. By conducting a SWOT analysis, you can break down the problem into manageable parts and examine each component in detail. As a result, SWOT can make the decision-making process less daunting and more manageable.

Moreover, conducting a SWOT analysis can help you to identify potential blind spots or biases that you may have. For example, when faced with a problem or decision, you may be biased toward a particular solution or approach. Conducting a SWOT analysis can help you identify any biases and ensure that you consider all options and perspectives before making a decision.

Additionally, conducting a SWOT analysis can help you to develop your problem-solving and critical-thinking skills. By examining a situation from different angles and considering all possible outcomes, you can build their ability to think critically and make informed decisions. It can help you to be more confident in your decision-making abilities, which can support them in being more courageous.

A SWOT analysis can help you build resilience and develop a growth mindset. You can work on these areas and develop new skills and abilities by identifying weaknesses and areas for improvement. This tool can help you become more resilient in facing challenges and setbacks. You will develop more confidence as you have the skills and abilities to overcome challenges and setbacks.

Let's use the following situation in business as an example:

It would help if you had a price increase for your service or product (i.e., garbage removal) due to the rise in gas prices and limitations related to the landfill. However, you are concerned that raising your prices will result in the loss of customers.

- S (strength): Your power is that your garbage is picked up four times a week at the same price as your competitor for picking up trash two times a week.
- W (weakness): Your weakness is that you are losing money.
- O (opportunities): You have opportunities to pick up garbage bins fewer times during the week like your competition, i.e., three times a week.
- T (threats): You face the threat of losing customers. However, the chances are minimal since you still pick up garbage more than your competitor.

The Fishbone Diagram (aka Ishikawa Diagram)

The fishbone diagram is another cause-and-effect methodology. Its methodology is very similar to the Five Whys, and to some extent, it incorporates them. Here you explore six categories regarding the potential cause for the lack of success. This methodology allows for a more in-depth investigation of concerns.

The categories can include:

- people
- environment
- material
- method
- machinery

Any of these categories can be altered to fit the situation.

The head of the fish is used to state the problem or opportunity. The bones of the fish represent the categories that may affect the outcome.

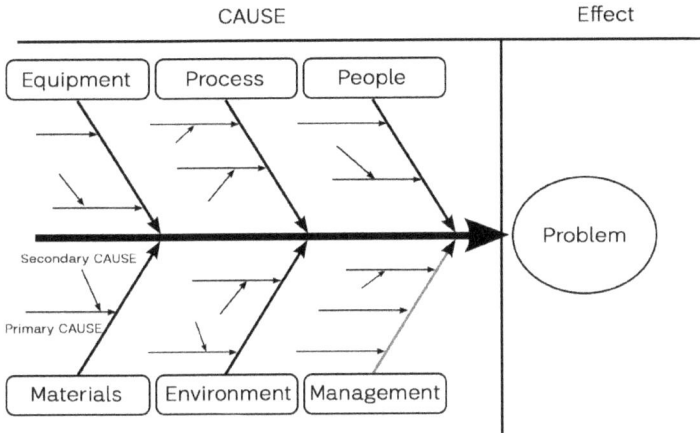

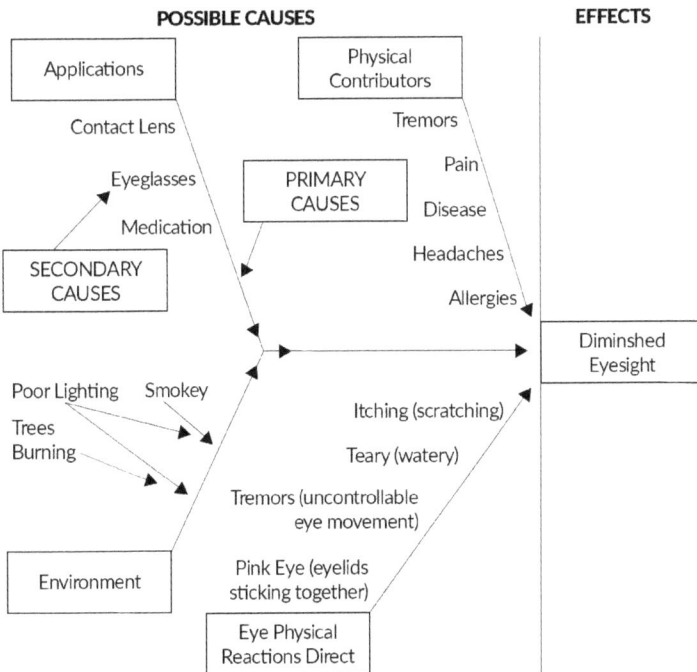

Advantages of using a Fishbone Diagram

Using the Ishikawa diagram can support being courageous in a few ways:

1. **Encouraging open communication:** The Fishbone diagram is a collaborative tool that involves multiple people from different backgrounds and perspectives. It encourages open communication and active participation from all members, which can help build trust and create a sense of psychological safety. This, in turn, can support being courageous by creating an environment where you feel comfortable sharing your ideas and perspectives.

2. **Identifying root causes:** The Fishbone diagram helps to identify the root causes of a problem or challenge. By understanding the underlying causes of a problem, you can be more courageous in addressing it. For example, if a company is experiencing low morale, the Fishbone diagram can help identify potential causes such as poor leadership, lack of recognition, or unclear expectations. Once the root causes are identified, you can be more courageous in addressing the issues head-on.

3. **Challenging assumptions:** The Fishbone diagram encourages you to challenge assumptions and explore alternative explanations. This can support being courageous by encouraging you to question the status quo and challenge conventional thinking.

4. **Facilitating problem-solving**: The Fishbone diagram is a structured problem-solving tool that guides you through a process of identifying, analyzing, and resolving problems. This can support being courageous by providing a clear framework for addressing complex issues and making decisions.

Disadvantages of using a Fishbone diagram

- Complex defects might yield many causes, which might become visually cluttering and paralyzing
- Interrelationships between causes are not easily identifiable
- It is important to remember that being courageous involves taking risks and facing potential failure or negative consequences. Using a Fishbone diagram to identify all potential risks and mitigations may lead to a tendency to focus too much on avoiding failure, which can stifle creativity and innovation.

Therefore, while a Fishbone diagram can be a useful tool in problem-solving, it is important to balance it with the need to take risks and be courageous in pursuit of your goals. It is essential to keep an open mind and be willing to embrace uncertainty and potential failure as a necessary part of the learning process.

Here is a more personal example of using a Fishbone diagram to make a courageous decision related to marriage. Should this couple terminate their marriage?

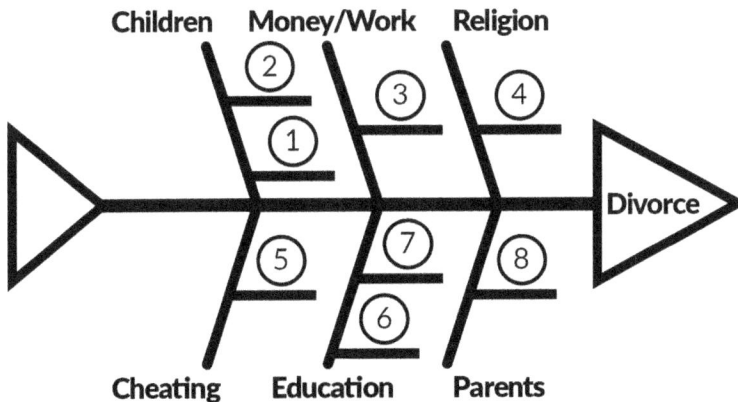

Causes

- **Children:** Still Living at home or financially dependent on parents as an adult
- **Money/work:** Not enough income to support the marriage
- **Religion:** Different religious faiths
- **Cheating:** Spouse travels 90% of the time out of state
- **Education:** Spouse wants to return to school resulting in an influx of friends from significantly higher academic circles
- **Spouse's Parents:** Live with the married couple resulting in different child-rearing principles

In this case, courage may be reflected in getting divorced or staying married and seeking spousal support.

Who killed the Plan?" I," said the Critic,
"I knew how to hit it, I killed the Plan."

Who killed the Plan "I," the Bore said.
"I talked it dead; I killed the Plan."

Who killed the Plan "I," said the Sloth.
"I lagged and was loth. And I killed the Plan."

Who killed the Plan? "I," said Ambition.
"With my selfish vision I killed the Plan."

Who killed the Plan? "I," said the Crank,
"With my nonsense rank I killed the Plan."

—Amos Russel Wells

SECTION 3

Poems and Quotes of Courage

The Spoken Word

This chapter aims to offer you words of wisdom to inspire and support your acts of Microcourage©. These words of wisdom have inspired my acts of Microcourage©, both in business and my personal life. My hope for you is that they will empower you to go for the gold and not for the silver or bronze.

"Great things are done by a series of small things brought together."
—Vincent Van Gogh

====

"Some people believe holding on and hanging in there are signs of great strength. However, there are times when it takes much more strength to know when to let go and then do it."
—Ann Landers

====

"I never lose. I either win or learn."
—Nelson Mandela

====

"The answer is the beginning of the question."
—CB Bowman-Ottomanelli

====

"There are no secrets to success.
It is the result of preparation, hard work,
and learning from failure."

—Colin Powell

====

"Start where you are, with what you have. Make
something of it and never be satisfied."

—George Washington Carver

====

"Courage doesn't always roar. Sometimes courage is
the little voice at the end of the day that says I'll try
again tomorrow."

—Mary Anne Radmacher

====

"The ultimate measure of a man is not where he
stands in moments of comfort and convenience,
but where he stands at times of challenge and
controversy."

—Martin Luther King Jr.

====

"Life is not a spectator sport. If you're going
to spend your whole life in the grandstand
just watching what goes on, in my opinion
you're wasting your life."

—Jackie Robinson

====

"Success is a journey, not a destination. The doing is often more important than the outcome."

—Arthur Ashe

====

"Just because you are happy it does not mean that the day is perfect but that you have looked beyond its imperfections."

—Bob Marley

====

"You must be willing to do what others won't do, to have what others won't have."

—Les Brown

====

"You take on the responsibility for making your dream a reality."

—Les Brown

====

"Courage is always within us; the question is when will we display it."

—CB Bowman-Ottomanelli

====

"Whatever we believe about ourselves and our ability comes true for us."

—Susan L. Taylor

====

"Success is to be measured not so much by the position that one has reached in life as by the obstacles which he has overcome while trying to succeed."

—Booker T. Washington

====

"I have discovered in life that there are ways of getting almost anywhere you want to go, if you really want to go."

—Langston Hughes

====

"Courage is simple solutions to complex problems."

—CB Bowman-Ottomanelli

====

"Never be limited by other people's limited imaginations."

—Dr. Mae Jemison

====

"It takes a great deal of bravery to stand up to our enemies, but just as much to stand up to our friends."

—J.K. Rowling, Harry Potter and the Sorcerer's Stone

====

"Microcourage© is acknowledging and respecting the courage you have within you."

—CB Bowman - Ottomanelli

====

"You have to believe in yourself when no one else does- that makes you a winner right there."

—Nelson Mandela

====

*"Some people like to think In-The-Box. Others, Out-Of-The-Box.
I prefer to think Without-Box, draw the boxes myself... and redraw them further."*

—Maïna K. M'Poyo

====

"I believe that the only courage anybody ever needs is the courage to follow your own dreams."

—Oprah Winfrey

====

"The moment I said yes to the challenge, the moment I was open to having the conversations, suddenly in that instance my life was changed. I grew more courageous; I shed some shyness, some awkwardness, some social fear."

—Shonda Rhimes

====

"I learned that courage was not the absence of fear, but the triumph over it."

—Nelson Mandela

====

"Courage is the most important of all the virtues, because without courage you can't practice any other virtue consistently."

—Maya Angelou

====

"It is curious that physical courage should be so common in the world and moral courage so rare."

—Mark Twain

====

"I learned that courage was not the absence of fear, but the triumph over it. The brave man is not he who does not feel afraid, but he who conquers that fear."

—Nelson Mandela

====

"Courage is in the eye of the beholder."

—CB Bowman-Ottomanelli

====

"Failure is an opportunity, it provides a university of knowledge" ©

—CB Bowman-Ottomanelli

SECTION 4

Et Cetera

The Lady Sings

"You've got the courage to Leap
You've got the courage to Lead
You're fierce and fearless
To be more —step out, stand tall
Know you're invincible
Be brave and be bold. Let it roar
Be brave and be bold. Let it roar"

—Courage to Leap & Lead Anthem

"Have courage to stand <u>up</u>, stand <u>alone</u>,
and the courage to <u>lead</u> by trying again."

—CB Bowman

This book was written so that everyone understands and acknowledges that we all have courage and that courage is experienced every day of our lives. The Courage to Leap & Lead resides in our every breath. First, however, we must start by recognizing, accepting, and applauding our courage. Next, we must know we can brag about it, assuming we are not braggadocious. Then, using the lens of Microcourage©, we can see how obtainable courage is in our daily lives.

The journaling pages of the book allow you, the reader, to incorporate your own Microcourage© stories while you are in the inspiration zone from reading "Courage to Leap & Lead."

These exercises will supply you with your touchpoints of success to use in times of need. Experiences build super strength, putting you on a path to develop your courage continuously.

In times of doubt, concern, and fear, you can call upon your super-strengths to remind us to have the courage to leap and lead ourselves and others.

As humans, we tend to forget the pain related to past successes, and instead, we glorify our accomplishments. Instead, we need to remember the struggles that lead to these successes as the lessons learned, placing them in our "mental university" as class notes.

This book is an immersion guide for successful organizations and evolving individuals. The goal is to provide *mental fortitude* by using the seven-step roadmap.

The process inspires participants to go for the gold by finding courage *through simple solutions to complex problems©*. Using the proven seven-point roadmap, readers re-envisioning how they think about courage. It is no longer considered some huge unattainable accomplishment. Instead, failure is seen from a different viewpoint —allowing you to see it as an opportunity to move forward through the lessons you have learned.

During these critical times of need arising from experiencing a perfect storm from the collision of five pandemics: social justice, COVID-19 (and its mutations), mental health, economics, and the environment. We must isolate and recognize our acts of courage and say, *"job well done."* This isolation and recognition will supply the nutrients needed not only to survive but to holistically flourish every day, where your successes can be viewed as one **Macro**courage and not only as a collection of small acts of **Micro**courage©.

"Be brave and be bold. Let it roar"!

Homework: Looking Back to Move Forward

Project #1: Take It Step-By-Step:

Think of a situation as an adult when you felt afraid yet chose to face your fear. (e.g., "I had to speak in front of 250 people at a conference.")

_____

_____

_____

What did you observe, think, and feel at the time? (e.g., "I saw the audience and felt butterflies in my stomach and tongue-tied. I was hoping that the stage would open and swallow me.")

_____

_____

_____

What did you or the people around you say, think, and do to help you face your fear? (e.g., "They clapped when I walked on stage.")

_____

_____

_____

At what point did your fear start to go down? (e.g., "They smiled and cheered after my first statement.")

_____

_____

How did you feel afterward? (e.g., exhilarated and proud)

_____

_____

b) Now, think back on a situation in childhood in which you faced your fear. How was it the same or different from the first situation? (e.g., "I was at an amusement park.")

_____

_____

What did you observe, think, and feel at the time? (e.g., "I saw the roller coaster and felt butterflies in my stomach.")

_____

_____

What did you or the people around you say, think, and do to help you face your fear? (e.g., "I told myself that if other kids could go on it, so could I.")

_____

_____

At what point did your fear start to go down? (e.g., "When I was locked into my seat, fear was replaced with excitement.")

_____

_____

How did you feel afterward? (e.g., exhilarated and proud)

_____

_____

Finally, think of a situation you currently face that creates fear or anxiety. Do these situations relate to your childhood experience or a previous experience as an adult? (e.g., "I've been asked to lead a team to develop a new service.")

_____

_____

What are you most afraid of in your journey? (e.g., "My leadership of the team, and the failure of the new service.")

_____

_____

- Is there a way to apply the same skills you used in the two earlier situations to be more courageous in this situation? (e.g., gain team respect, gain team support.)

- Remind yourself that you have these skills and have used them successfully.

- What mental or environmental barriers stand in the way of using these skills? (e.g., "I've never led a team; I'm not sure the new service idea will be supported.")

- How can you cope with or get rid of these barriers? (e.g., attend Microcourage© University, obtain an executive coach, and use the tools presented in the book *Courage to Leap & Lead: A Roadmap to Redefine Failure Into Success.*)

Project #2: Create Make It Happen Team(s) (MIH)

These are teams that will support you in your courage project. Note that different courage projects may require other groups.

Identify your *MIH* teams by starting with the following parameters to screen participants:

- Who should be on your team?
- Why are they on your team (what do you admire about them)?
- What is their role?
- How will you hold them accountable?
- How will they hold you accountable?

Refer to the company and personal values, communication styles, and types below.

The Courage to Leap & Lead Values: Company vs. Personal

Company Values:

The internal beliefs, ethics, and guiding morals upon which a business bases it's objectives and business practices. Company values guide business owners and employees in making important decisions determining the organization's success.

A few examples of company values include:

- Accountability
- Boldness
- Collaboration
- Continuous improvement

- Curiosity
- Customer Commitment
- Diversity
- Honesty

- Humility
- Inclusion
- Innovation
- Integrity

Personal Values:

Leadership institutes and programs commonly use core values (personal values). However, this list is not exhaustive.

- Authenticity
- Achievement
- Adventure
- Authority
- Autonomy
- Balance
- Beauty
- Boldness
- Compassion
- Challenge
- Citizenship
- Community
- Kindness

- Knowledge
- Leadership
- Learning
- Love
- Loyalty
- Meaningful work
- Pleasure
- Poise
- Popularity
- Recognition
- Religion
- Reputation
- Respect

The Courage to Leap & Lead Communication Types

Verbal:

- Face-to-face
- Over the phone
- Through Skype or Zoom
- Chatting with friends or family

Non-Verbal:

- Eye contact
- Body language
- Facial expressions
- Tone of voice
- Posture
- Gestures

Written:

- Emails
- Reports
- Bulletins
- Letters
- Manuals
- Telegrams

Listening:

- Active listening is the key to all effective communication

Visual:

- Images
- Infographics
- Videos
- Visual presentations

Project #3: Courage Project

1. Identify your *"Courage Project."*

Thinking back over the last six months, what is the one thing you wish you dared to do but did not do? For Example:

- Launch a company
- Get a dog
- Get a degree
- Deal with a problem child
- Join a team
- Get divorced
- Launch a new service/ product
- Courage to go beyond past failures

2. What do you feel is holding you back? e.g.,

- Fear
- Education/ knowledge
- Money
- Connections
- Support
- Time
- Family
- Beliefs
- Exposure

1. Which Microcourage© tool will you use to start?
2. How and when will you reward yourself?
3. Identify your MIH team.
4. Begin your journey using your roadmap!
5. Enjoy the adventure. Learn from your experience.
6. Identify lessons learned.

The Epilogue

Our uncertainty and fear have bubbled up to the surface due to the current five pandemics trying to drown us. The result is that our system thinking for solving anxiety has gone askew. However, through the use of the Microcourage©, tools and patterns borrowed from systems thinkers, we can identify and abort what is stopping us from reaching our goals.

As an executive, having the courage to make difficult decisions and take calculated risks can be crucial to your company's success. In addition, building the confidence to act on your convictions will be invaluable. A courageous leader is not afraid to challenge the status quo, speak their truth, and take action in the face of uncertainty.

Courageous leadership can inspire and motivate teams, foster a culture of innovation, and ultimately drive business growth. It is a powerful personal and professional development tool and can help you and your team tap into your full creative and leadership potential.

Final Thoughts

The Cocoon

A man found a cocoon of an emperor moth and took it home to watch it emerge.

One day a small opening appeared, and for several hours the moth struggled, but it couldn't seem to force its body past a certain point.

Deciding something was wrong, the man took the scissors and snipped the remaining bit of cocoon.

The moth emerged easily, its body large and swollen, the wings small and shriveled.

He expected that in a few hours the wings would spread out in their natural beauty, but they did not.

Instead of developing into a creature free to fly, the moth spent its life dragging around a swollen body and shriveled wings.

The constricting cocoon and the struggle necessary to pass through the tiny opening are nature's way of forcing fluid from the body into the wings.

The 'merciful' snip was in reality, cruel. Sometimes the struggle is exactly what we need. Struggles lead to great success.

SECTION 5

Extras

The Gift

C ongratulations on purchasing and reading "Courage to Leap & Lead: A Roadmap for Redefining Failure Into Courage." Reading this book demonstrates a commitment to growth and continuous learning for you and those who respect and are inspired by you.

There's a gift in every challenge and a lesson in every setback; you have the strength and wisdom to recognize this but does your leadership team in your organization? I want to share with your teams the gift I've found through years of dedicated study and real-world application of the secrets of inspiring Courageous Leadership. Courageous Leadership is not just about taking risks or making bold decisions. It's about fostering a culture that encourages authenticity, transparency, and integrity. It's about leading by example and inspiring others to do the same. It's about aggregating trust as a thought leader. In a rapidly changing business landscape, Courageous Leadership is not just a nicety - it's a necessity.

My gift to you and your organization is that I will spend 1.5 hours virtually with your senior leaders, imparting valuable insights and helping to cultivate the seeds of Courageous Leadership in your organization. We will work collaboratively to chart a course for your company's future, and I guarantee you'll see the immediate benefits.

In my book, I've laid out a systematic approach to nurturing Courageous Leadership and practical exercises to drive the concepts home. The most effective way to implement these principles is to ensure every team member has access to this knowledge and has completed the exercises in the book.

To maximize our time together and ensure everyone is on the same page, I request that you provide each participant with a copy of my book and that they have read and completed the exercises before our meeting.

By investing in Courageous Leadership, you're investing in your company's future. The payoffs offer improved relationships with stakeholders and customers and a stronger, more cohesive team ready to face whatever challenges lie ahead.

Should you have any questions or require further clarification, please do not hesitate to contact me at cb@cbbowman.com.

The possibilities are endless by believing in the power of courage and Leadership. Courageously Yours, C.B. Bowman-Ottomanelli

Certification

The Microcourage© process is a personal and professional development methodology emphasizing self-awareness, reflection, and accountability. It is a powerful tool for individuals and organizations seeking to enhance their leadership, communication, and problem-solving skills, in addition to being able to increase their capacity for innovation and creativity.

Becoming certified in the Microcourage© process can provide numerous benefits, including increased credibility, enhanced skills, and building your courage muscle. One of the most significant benefits of becoming certified using the Microcourage© process is increased reliability and credibility *as a leader*. In addition, certification demonstrates that an individual has a thorough understanding of building, supporting, and rewarding courage and has shown the ability to apply it effectively.

This knowledge can be especially valuable for coaching, consulting, and training professionals, where credibility and expertise are essential to building a successful practice. Additionally, certification can help individuals stand out in a crowded market, differentiate themselves from competitors, and increase their earning potential.

Another benefit of becoming certified in using the Microcourage© process is enhanced skills. The process is designed to help individuals develop a range of competencies, including emotional intelligence, communication, and problem-solving. Under certification, individuals can deepen their understanding of these skills and gain practical experience applying them. This training can be particularly valuable for professionals seeking to enhance their leadership skills, as the Microcourage process emphasizes self-awareness and accountability, two critical components of effective leadership.

Certification in using the Microcourage process can also provide access to a supportive community of practitioners. The Microcourage Institute, the organization that oversees certification, offers a range of resources and networking opportunities for certified practitioners. This community can provide ongoing support, mentorship, and opportunities for collaboration, which can be especially valuable for leaders and potential leaders looking to expand their trusted professional network.

In addition to these specific benefits, becoming certified using the Microcourage© process can also benefit individuals and organizations. The approach emphasizes self-awareness, reflection, and accountability, which can help individuals develop a more comprehensive understanding of themselves and their goals. As a result, the training can lead to increased clarity, purpose, and direction in both personal and professional contexts.

For organizations, certification in the Microcourage process can effectively build a culture of accountability and continuous improvement. In addition, organizations can embed the process into their operations by training a team of certified practitioners and creating a shared language and framework for personal and professional development. Finally, this process can foster a culture of innovation, collaboration, and adaptability, which is especially valuable in today's rapidly changing business landscape.

The Microcourage© certification program supports leaders in automatically applying the six-step roadmap to complex problems and opportunities, from relaunching a product or service to team building to resolving life's challenges, thus saving vast amounts of time and money wandering in a non-productive space.

It is important to note that becoming certified using the Microcourage© process is not a silver bullet. Like any tool or methodology, it is only as effective as the individual or organization using it. Therefore, certification does not guarantee success, and it is up to the individual to apply the process effectively and consistently. However, for individuals and organizations committed to personal and professional development, certification in the Microcourage© process can be a powerful tool for achieving their goals.

The intention is for this process to become a way of life. Therefore, becoming certified as a "Microcourage© Master Trainer" is recommended for all who wish to apply the principles presented in this book to create a shift in mindset —"expanding the possibilities," to quote Dr. Ana Melikian.

Program Features:

- Class sizes appropriate to your need
- Certified instructors
- A psychological safe space
- Expertise in the use of tools presented in this book and more
- Multiple opportunities to practice and receive positive feedback
- Post-program individual coaching and consulting sessions
- Access to all of the resources, videos, and guides for free or discounted prices
- Access to conferences and new workshops at a discounted price.

Key Takeaways:

- How to use the Microcourage© process effectively and efficiently
- How to embed the process with key stakeholders
- How to use the process to change key outcomes
- How to expedite ramping up for launches and relaunches
- How to leverage the process to change the dialogue

Contact us at Microcourage© University for details on how to bring us to your organization and how to become certified:

https://courage-consulting.com/;
info@courage-consulting.com

Recommendations

Goldsmith, M., & Reiter, M. (2022). *Earned life: Lose regret, choose fulfillment.* Doubleday

Goldsmith, M., & Reiter, M. (2015). *Triggers creating behavior that lasts, becoming the person you want to be.* Crown Publishing Group

Goldsmith, M., & Reiter, M. (2007). *What Got You Here Won't Get You There: How Successful People Become Even More Successful.* Hachette Books

Dr. Deborah Gilboa (2022) *From Stressed to Resilient: The Guide to Handle More and Feel It Less.* CNS Publishing

Dr. Rita McGrath (2019). *Seeing Around Corners: How to Spot Inflection Points in Business Before They Happen.* Harper Business

Edgar Papke (2015) *The Elephant in the Boardroom: How Leaders Use and Manage Conflict to Reach Greater Levels of Success.* Weiser

Brené Brown (2017) Braving the Wilderness: The Quest for True Belonging and the Courage to Stand Alone. Random House

Gregg Ward, MCEC, BCC (2022) *Restoring Respect...A "how-to" guide for supporting the repair of broken work relationships."* Winding Creek Press/ The Center for Respectful Leadership

Dr. Amy Cuddy, *Presence: (2015) Bringing Your Boldest Self to Your Biggest Challenges*. Little, Brown, and Company

Sally Helgesen, Foreword by Marshall Goldsmith *(2023) Rising Together How We Can Bridge Divides and Create a More Inclusive Workplace*. Hachette Book Group (HBG)

About the Author

CB Bowman-Ottomanelli,
MCEC, CMC, BCC, CVP, CVF

Meet CB Bowman, author, keynote speaker, workshop leader, consultant, and host of "Courage: To Leap & Lead" videocast and podcast.

CB Bowman-Ottomanelli went from being a victim of corporate racism to the CEO of Courage Consulting, helping organizations implement courage through simple solutions to complex problems and recognizing the power of Microcourage©.

She is also the founder and CEO of the change-making organization in the coaching field, the Association of Corporate Executive Coaches.

CB brings clarity and accountability to the world of executive coaching. She founded the change-making organization in the coaching field, the Association of Corporate Executive Coaches© (ACEC). The association is dedicated to master-level coaches who are working with the top tier of organizations. It offers the acclaimed MCEC (Master Corporate Executive Coach Certification) through the MEECO Leadership Institute.

CB believes that master-level corporate executive coaches must be "enterprise-wide business partners©" with their clients. She is also the force behind the powerful dialogue-based ACEC Leadership Conferences that biennially present executive coaches with the latest forward-thinking tools.

She is formally head of branding for ready-to-eat cereals for General Foods, where she was responsible for the visual impact of Post Cereals for iconic brands such as Honey Bunches of Oats, Honey Golden Crisps, and Fruity Pebbles. CB was also responsible for classic brands, including Post Shredded Wheat, Grape Nuts, Shake 'n Bake, and Raisin Bran, taking home several awards for product branding. In addition, she was part of the successful branding for the Birds Eye frozen food product line and was responsible for the visual branding merger of Nabisco's ready-to-eat Cereals into the Post line of Cereals.

CB has been a guest speaker and panelist for Renaissance Weekend, named one of the Power List of the Top 200 Biggest Voices in Leadership by Leadershum; Top 50 coaches in the world by Thinkers50; Global Gurus also named her as one of the top 15 experts in branding and ranked by Marshall Goldsmith Top Global Coaches as the #1 coach for increasing the quality of coaching. CB is also a "Certified Master Corporate Executive Coach."

Her keynotes and workshops, "The Courage to Leap & Lead," inspire others to go for the gold by finding courage through simple solutions to complex problems. And by re-envisioning how they think about courage —in terms of profitability and a willingness to see failure as a success.

She also co-founded the National Association for Interior Designers and was Chairperson for the North Plainfield, New Jersey's Historic Commission, for six years.

CB is a graduate of the New School for Social Research, which she proudly states was the best formal education she received. She received her MBA from Pace University, where she served on the Advisory board for the Lubin School of Business as an adjunct professor in the marketing department. In addition, she served as an instructor at Rutgers University Center for Management Development and as an adjunct professor at Mercy College, teaching Organizational Behavior and Human Resource Management.

She is a contributing author in the *"Complex Situations in Coaching: A Critical Case-Based Approach,"* 1st Edition, and she is also a contributing author for *"Coach Me! Your Personal Board of Directors: Leadership Advice from the World's Greatest Coaches."* and has published several articles on coaching. Her book *"Courage to Leap & Lead"*... A Roadmap for Redefining Failure Into Success is expected to be released in June 2023.

TRANSFORMATION AFFILIATIONS:

Renaissance Weekend • Thinkers50 • Global Gurus • Stakeholder Centered Coaching (SCC) by Dr. Marshall Goldsmith, Ph.D. • Master Certified Coach (CMC) by The Behavioral Institute • Board Certified Coach (BCC) by the Center for Credentialing & Education • Master Corporate Executive Coach (MCEC) by the MEECO Leadership Institute • LinkedIn Live broadcaster • Apple Podcast broadcaster

- Awardee: Thinkers 360: Top 10 Thought Leader in Diversity & Inclusion; Top 50 Thought Leader in Leadership; and Top 25 Thought Leader in Management;
- Certified Virtual Presenter (CVP)
- Certified Virtual Facilitator (CVF)
- Leadershum 200 Biggest Voices in Leadership
- Marshall Goldsmith Top 50 Global Coaches

www.ingramcontent.com/pod-product-compliance
Lightning Source LLC
Chambersburg PA
CBHW071219090426
42736CB00014B/2896